BAD BOYS

OF FASHION

STYLE REBELS AND
— RENEGADES —
THROUGH THE AGES

JENNIFER CROLL

ILLUSTRATED BY **ANETA PACHOLSKA**

annick press
toronto + berkeley

For my father, Andrew, and his purple plaid bell-bottoms. —*J.C.*

———————

Page 182 constitutes an extension of
this copyright page.
Cover art and title type by Aneta Pacholska
Cover and interior design by Emma Dolan
Edited by Paula Ayer

Annick Press Ltd.

We acknowledge the support of the Canada
Council for the Arts and the Ontario Arts Council,
and the participation of the Government of
Canada/la participation du gouvernement du
Canada for our publishing activities.

Cataloging in Publication

Croll, Jennifer, 1980-, author
    Bad boys of fashion : style rebels and
renegades through the ages / Jennifer
Croll ; illustrated by Aneta Pacholska.

ISBN 978-1-77321-243-2 (hardcover).
ISBN 978-1-77321-242-5 (softcover).
ISBN 978-1-77321-245-6 (HTML).
ISBN 978-1-77321-244-9 (PDF)

    1. Fashion—History—Juvenile literature.
2. Men's clothing—History—Juvenile literature.
3. Celebrities—Clothing—Juvenile literature.
4. Men—Biography—Juvenile literature.
5. Celebrities—Biography—Juvenile literature.
I. Pacholska, Aneta, illustrator
II. Title.

GT1710.C76 2019   j391'.10922   C2018-903731-8
                                  C2018-903732-6

Published in the U.S.A. by Annick Press (U.S.) Ltd.
Distributed in Canada by University of Toronto Press.
Distributed in the U.S.A. by Publishers Group West.

Printed in China

annickpress.com
jencroll.com
anetape.com

Also available as an e-book. Please visit annickpress.com/ebooks for more details.

CONTENTS

INTRODUCTION

WHEN YOU THINK about men's clothing, what do you imagine? A dark-colored suit? Jeans and a T-shirt? Those might be obvious answers, but there are lots of other options: safety-pinned leather pants, bright-pink tailored suits, team jerseys, metallic purple jumpsuits with plunging necklines, preppy polo shirts—or even dresses. Some men like to blend in, while others like to stand out, and there's a dizzying variety of ways sartorial rebels can make their mark, whether they choose a pair of brightly colored high-tops or a bedazzled one-piece. So why do we tend to think of men's clothing in such limited ways?

Up until just over two hundred years ago, men's fashion was far more showy than it is today. Colorful tights, billowy pantaloons, high heels, flowing coats in luxurious fabrics, and large, curly wigs were all considered mainstream men's fashion. Being able to dress decadently was a sign that a man had money, and in general, having money meant having power and status. Show-offy fashion, for men, was a way to demonstrate that they were important.

Men only began to dress more simply after the French Revolution and the Industrial Revolution, both of which created massive social change in the late eighteenth century. The French Revolution violently overthrew the monarchy as well as all of its symbols—including fancy dress. Meanwhile, the Industrial Revolution's booming factories created a large middle class of working men who needed practical clothing for their jobs. By the early nineteenth century, the aesthetic of a stylish man had entirely changed from an over-the-top, colorful peacock to a somber, dark-colored silhouette.

But that wasn't the end of it. That simple uniform ended up being something rebellious men could reject, play with, or replace. The dandies of the nineteenth century polished and perfected stylish dress, adopting crisp tailored suits and elegant accessories. And partway into the twentieth century, growing wealth and the end of child labor helped create an entirely new class in society: teenagers. Before that point, children had moved directly into adulthood and all its responsibilities, but beginning roughly in the 1940s, they spent more years in school, were given allowances, and had spare time to do what they wanted—which often meant misbehaving and rejecting the culture of their parents. New youth subcultures kept appearing, each one with edgy new fashions: greasers with jeans and leather jackets, hippies with bell-bottoms and tie-dye, punks with torn T-shirts and Mohawks. These subcultural styles allowed teenage boys to prove they were nothing like their boring parents just by putting on a new outfit.

Teenagers weren't the only ones shaking up menswear in the twentieth century. Civil rights movements were pushing for racial equality, gay rights, and sexual equality—and as they did, they brought with them unique fashions that had been growing and thriving in oppressed communities into the mainstream. The end of segregation meant that African American fashion trends, like zoot suits and, later, hip hop fashion, were soon worn by everyone. Dressing ultra-fashionably or androgynously— as some gay men did—became more accepted in the straight community. And the women's movement, with its push for the equality of the sexes, criticized the idea that beauty and fashion were uniquely female obsessions, freeing them up to be adopted by men; if women could spend time on their appearances, men could, too. By the early twenty-first century, many people rejected the idea that gender was a binary between male and female—meaning that gender-nonconforming dress might not just indicate a man in rebellion, but a person defining their gender in a way that makes sense to them.

Today, a teenager might still wear the jeans and T-shirt that a 1950s greaser did, but he's got choices thanks to the rebellious fashion icons in this book who changed the definition of menswear with their own non-conformist choices. If he thinks of himself as a rule-breaking outsider, that teen could spike his hair and wear a torn punk T-shirt like Malcolm McLaren, or if he considers himself a cultural critic, put on a natty suit and tie and pretend he's a witty nineteenth-century aesthete like Oscar Wilde—or the modern equivalent, a hipster. He could prep up his image with a pink polo shirt like a young Kanye West or really push some boundaries with a kilt, like a latter-day West. Or if he's a real bad boy, he could throw on a leather jacket, jeans, and motorcycle boots like Marlon Brando. Throughout the pages of this book, McLaren, Wilde, West, Brando, and twenty-six other famous men prove that men's fashion is as varied and interesting as the lives men lead and, most of all, that clothes have meaning—just like those rich eighteenth-century guys in tights and curly wigs did, men today use clothing to tell the world what they're all about. ◆

CHAPTER ONE

LOUIS XIV
FASHION RULER

FULL NAME Louis-Dieudonné de Bourbon

BORN September 5, 1638,
Saint-Germain-en-Laye, France

DIED September 1, 1715, Versailles, France

OCCUPATION King of France

BAD BOY CRED Opulent fashion helped Louis XIV
claim power and keep it

In front of the rapt crowd watching the court ballet, a young man dances on a dark stage, barely lit by a silvery light. As he dances, he sings: "The sun following me is young Louis. All the stars will flee once the great king advances!" Then the stage becomes brighter, and a figure dances out. He wears a skirt of golden feathers, golden tights, golden shoes, and, on his head, a golden crown in the shape of a sun. The crowd collectively gasps, and from the back of the theater, some people start yelling. "Vive le roi!" they call. "Long live the king!"

Louis XIV was known as the Sun King, a name he chose to associate himself with godly power and divine beauty. He reigned over France for seventy-two years, a period of prosperity and stability often referred to as "le Grand Siècle" (the Great Century), in which he cemented his country's status as the leading European power. One of the ways he communicated and held on to power was through fashion. Louis dressed in an elaborate, ornate, and expensive manner meant to make him look more like a god than a man. At the same time, he set sartorial rules that positioned France to become the world's center of fashion.

THE LITTLE KING

FOR LOUIS, THERE was never any doubt about what path his life would take. His greatness was ordained. He was the eldest son of Louis XIII, the King of France, which meant that according to succession rules he, too, would be king someday. At the time of his birth, there was a great deal of anxiety about whether his mother would deliver a boy or a girl; only a son could be heir to the throne. So when Louis was born, his parents were so overjoyed that they named him Louis-Dieudonné—French for "gift of God."

Louis took his name to heart. When he was officially baptized, at age four and a half, he was dressed in a flowing silver gown, and afterward, he was taken to see his father, who was ill. His father, the king, asked Louis what his name was. Louis replied, "Louis the fourteenth." His father told him, "Not yet, but soon." Two months later, the senior Louis passed away,

A teenage Louis posing in his coronation robes.

and Louis-Dieudonné became King Louis XIV. He wasn't even five years old. Of course, a small child can't rule a country, and so his mother, the queen, acted as regent until he was old enough to rule.

Louis came of age when he turned thirteen, and he made a formal procession to parliament to declare his assumption of power. Accompanied by a royal cavalcade adorned in red and white feathers, he rode through Paris on horseback, wearing a richly embroidered suit so ornate that viewers compared him to "a young Apollo." All along the way, crowds cheered him on, yelling, *"Vive le roi!"* However, his official coronation was delayed for almost two years, mostly due to military conflicts in northern France.

For Louis, those two years were spent making an impression on his subjects.

APOLLO

In Greek mythology, Apollo was an important god who was associated with the arts, poetry, medicine, and the sun. Since ancient times, Apollo has been a popular subject for artists, who have usually depicted him as a handsome young man—sometimes accompanied by sun imagery.

SONG AND DANCE MAN

An etching of Louis XIV dressed as Apollo.

AT THE TIME of Louis's reign, court ballets were staged for the purposes of entertainment—and propaganda. These ballets weren't like the ballets of today. They did involve dancing, but they also incorporated singing, poetry, and elaborate sets and costumes. The roles were all played by monarchs and members of their court, but the performances were staged in public, so anyone could come. Because of that, they offered opportunities for rulers to present themselves in a flattering light before ordinary people.

When he was fourteen years old, in 1653, Louis performed in a thirteen-hour-long court ballet called *Ballet de la Nuit*. The timing was important; from 1648 to 1653, France had been embroiled in a series of civil wars called the Fronde, in which the French nobility rose up against the monarchy. Louis and his forces ultimately won, but the experience made him distrust the aristocracy and more determined to prove his absolute power. Dressed in an over-the-top golden costume, Louis played the role of Apollo, or, as he was named in the ballet, the Sun King. The ballet's message was clear—Louis was a sort of god whose power should be respected. Forever after, he was associated with the divine, and became known as the Sun King.

Midway into his reign, Louis moved his court from Paris to Versailles, a residence just outside of Paris that he spent a fortune on transforming into an expansive, glittering palace, full of mirrors and silver. He pressured the nobility to spend time there—if they were at court, Louis could keep them under control. At Versailles, court life became a performance as elaborate as a ballet. Nobles wanted to get close to the king—often during his *lever*—but there was a dress code required for attendance at Versailles. Louis issued an edict declaring that all his courtiers had to be fashionable. Men were required to wear a silk or velvet coat, covered in embroidery and jewels, called a *habit habillé*. The higher a man ranked, the more elaborately he

LEVER AND COUCHER

Dressing and undressing was a highly ritualized performance for Louis XIV. During his *lever* (rising), Louis would welcome visitors into his chamber while he dressed, beginning with those closest to him in terms of power and influence. While the tradition existed before Louis, he transformed it into a spectacle, and a formal one, too: courtiers weren't granted an audience with the king unless they were dressed in their finest clothing. The entire procedure, which began when the curtains of his bed were thrown back and ended with him heading to mass, took about an hour and a half. He had a similar procedure at night, called a *coucher*.

was expected to dress. A room full of courtiers was like a showcase for the French fashion industry, as Louis had banned all foreign-made clothing—a rule that immediately increased business for French fashion. Dressing this way was extraordinarily expensive, and some thought that Louis's rules were another way to keep courtiers at bay—if they were spending all their money on clothing and spending all their time at court, they wouldn't have the time or resources to rebel against him.

Above: Examples of court fashion during Louis XIV's reign.

IT'S 8:00 A.M. Inside the bedroom at Versailles, the curtains on a four-poster bed are drawn back to reveal the king. Several attendants rush to help him remove his shirt and put on a fresh one. Soon there is a crowd gathered as the king shaves; dons a beautiful frock coat; puts on a long, curly black wig; and pulls on his gloves. Finally, he showily pulls silk stockings over his legs and slides his feet into shoes with diamond buckles and red heels.

IF THE SHOE FITS

OF COURSE, LOUIS set the bar with what he wore himself. At the point that Louis came to power, Spanish fashions were in vogue—and the Spaniards wore rigid, black, somber clothing. Louis overturned all of that with his brightly colored, over-the-top attire. He would wear silk and satin coats, silk stockings held up by garters, French-lace shirts, a curly black wig, and red high heels. His collection of clothing was so expansive and elaborate that he had to hire a fashion director, or *grand maître de la garde-robe*, to manage his wardrobe, which was stored in several different rooms. He had an official shoemaker, too, who designed high heels that were meant to make him look taller (Louis was only five four, and he felt the extra height helped him look more kinglike) and accentuate his stocking-clad legs, which Louis considered to be one of his good features. The shoes had red heels, often about four inches high, which were sometimes engraved with battle scenes. Louis decreed that only members of his court could wear red heels, and after that, red heels became a status symbol for men.

The wig that Louis wore also sparked a trend, and long, curly wigs—which weren't cheap—became another class marker. Long hair for men had already been in fashion, however, and Louis adopted a wig for reasons other than style. His hair began thinning when he was only seventeen years old, likely due to syphilis, a very common sexually transmitted disease that at the time had no cure. One of the symptoms of syphilis was baldness, and Louis, worried that a bald head would tarnish his reputation, commissioned a grand wig to hide it. The ploy worked, and rather than being seen as a cover-up, a wig became de rigueur.

In order to make sure everyone knew how grand and powerful he was, Louis turned to printed propaganda. He created a printmaking department within the monarchy and employed France's best etchers and engravers to help record his likeness. The prints, which depicted Louis, as well as important festivals and military victories, were given as gifts to foreign rulers and sold at French

HIGH HEELS

High heels were originally designed for Persian soldiers who fought on horseback; the heels helped them stand up in their stirrups so they could shoot bows and arrows. Eventually the trend caught on in Europe. Because they were military garb, high heels were associated with masculinity, and men wore them to look more virile. Soon they were worn by men of all classes, and the aristocracy set themselves apart by adopting heels that were higher and more impractical. Women only began wearing high heels later—to give their outfits a masculine edge.

Right: Louis XIV pointing a toe in his famous red heels.

markets. Louis also produced a series of medallions engraved with his likeness, which circulated through French society. This meant that everyone had a certain picture of Louis in their minds: an image that had been carefully tailored by Louis to make himself appear as impressive and kingly as possible. Distributing prints of his likeness also helped popularize the king's fashion style.

Over the years Louis was in power, French fashion spread across the European continent, and soon, people were dressing like Louis everywhere from Spain to England. The proliferation of French fashion across Europe cemented France as the center of the fashion industry: due to Louis, French fabrics and designs were considered to be the best, and the increased demand created jobs in a myriad of fashion-related fields. Today, France still holds a position of dominance in the global fashion industry, all thanks to what Louis started.

Louis's reign marked the peak of extravagant men's fashion. Not long

Left: A medallion bearing Louis XIV's image.

A SMALL GROUP of people cluster around a booth in the crowded Paris market. They pass between them a piece of paper, which bears an illustration of a pompous-looking man posing with flowing curly hair and high heels. "His shoes are exquisite," one says. "I should buy this. Then I can show my cobbler what good shoes really look like!"

after his death in 1715, the tide turned. The French Revolution in 1789 toppled the aristocracy headed by Louis's grandson, Louis XVI. During the violent years afterward, clothing was considered an important way to show your political affiliation—and dressing like the aristocracy was dangerous. Members of the aristocracy were guillotined, and clothing that signified noble status, like silks, velvets, and taffetas, was banned. The Industrial Revolution, which began in 1769, had an even more pronounced effect. Prior to that, fashion had largely been dictated by the upper classes, but the factory jobs of the Industrial Revolution popularized streamlined fashions for the new middle class. Gone were elaborate robes, frilly shirts, silk stockings, and buckled shoes, and in their place were simple, practical, dark-colored suits. This shift was so dramatic that it even has a name: the Great Masculine Renunciation.

Though men today don't dress anything like him, Louis had a huge influence on modern fashion.

Typical French fashion from the end of Louis XIV's reign.

The rules he created for the dress of courtiers and French suppliers turned France into the world's dominant fashion power, a role it has never given up. More than that, King Louis XIV proved that fashion isn't frivolous: it's a potent tool that helped him communicate power to whoever looked his way. ◆

FASHION SPOTLIGHT

NELSON MANDELA

FULL NAME: Nelson Rolihlahla Mandela

BORN: July 18, 1918, Mvezo, Union of South Africa

DIED: December 5, 2013, Johannesburg, South Africa

OCCUPATION: Revolutionary, political leader, president of South Africa

BAD BOY CRED: Mandela's patterned Madiba shirts proved he was a different kind of leader.

REJECTION OF AUTHORITY was Nelson Mandela's political trademark. The former revolutionary leader who became South Africa's president brought that same ethos to his fashion, making what other world leaders wore look boring, conservative, and predictable.

Despite his later rebellion, Mandela was actually born into royalty: he was part of the royal family of the Thembu tribe in South Africa. As a child, he was given the name Rolihlahla, which means "troublemaker"; he only became "Nelson" when he attended a missionary school run by

Methodists. (He later became known as "Madiba," the name of his clan.) Mandela excelled at school and went on to complete a B.A. in English and attend law school. While at law school, he became involved with the African National Congress (ANC). At the time, South Africa was ruled under apartheid, a political system of racial segregation and discrimination. The ANC was a political group that fought segregation, but during Mandela's time, they turned to violence to achieve their goals. Mandela led the ANC's militant wing through a series of bombings that sabotaged government structures, and in 1962, he was captured and went through two trials. At the first, he made a statement by wearing a traditional kaross (animal skin cloak) and beaded necklaces— "I knew well the authorities would feel threatened by my kaross as so many whites felt threatened by the true culture of Africa," he later wrote in his autobiography. At the second trial, he made a four-hour political speech rather than defend himself.

He told the court that he was ready to die for a democratic, racially free society—but rather than a death sentence, he was given life in prison.

Behind bars, Mandela became internationally famous as a political prisoner, and "Free Mandela!" was a well-known slogan. In 1990—twenty-six years after Mandela went to

Mandela in his kaross.

Mandela visiting the White House in one of his Madiba shirts.

prison—South Africa's president determined that it was time to end apartheid, and as recognition of that fact, he released Mandela from prison. Apartheid was officially over in 1991, and four years later, in the first election in which black South Africans could vote, Mandela became the country's first black president.

As president, Mandela reportedly turned down an offer to be dressed by pricey Italian fashion designer Giorgio Armani, and instead chose a wardrobe of his own creation. After receiving a gift of patterned shirts from President Suharto of Indonesia, Mandela was inspired to make some of his own. His versions were custommade from boldly patterned Javanese silk or African fabrics; featured a stiff collar, long sleeves, and a long cut; and were worn untucked. Mandela's own tailor made the first versions, but he later procured others from local South African designers. In South Africa, men didn't wear suits, and Mandela wanted to be both relatable and recognizable—these shirts were his own, a more casual uniform that communicated a new kind of leadership to South Africans. Mandela's flamboyant shirts became widely known as "Madiba shirts," in reference to Mandela's nickname. Mandela said that in comparison to wearing a suit and tie, his Madiba shirts made him feel free—an important sartorial statement for a man who spent his whole life fighting for freedom. ◆

ICONIC LOOK
JAWAHARLAL NEHRU

Jawaharlal Nehru was India's first prime minister after the country achieved independence from British colonial rule. He was in power for seventeen years and was beloved enough to earn the nickname "Uncle Nehru." Nehru distinguished himself from the suit-wearing colonial rulers of India by wearing a traditional Indian garment called an achkan—a knee-length jacket with buttons and a rounded collar worn by the region's royals for centuries—which he paired with a cap like the one popularized by Gandhi. Nehru's jacket sparked a trend, and a shorter, modified version became popular around the world in the 1960s. Referred to as a Nehru jacket, it's still a fashion staple today.

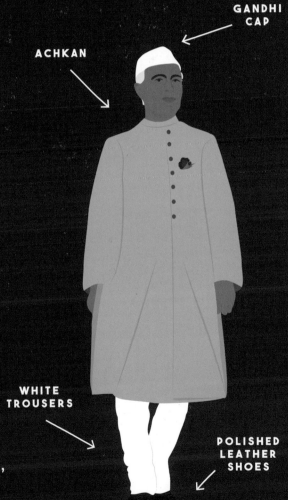

GANDHI CAP

ACHKAN

WHITE TROUSERS

POLISHED LEATHER SHOES

CHAPTER TWO

OSCAR WILDE

FASHION AESTHETE

FULL NAME: Oscar Fingal O'Flahertie Wills Wilde

BORN: October 16, 1854, Dublin, Ireland

DIED: November 30, 1900, Paris, France

OCCUPATION: Poet, playwright

BAD BOY CRED: Wilde lived for beauty in his life, writing, and fashion—even when it put him in danger.

Inside the arched door of the imposing London building, the crowd buzzes. People are here to attend the opening of the brand-new Grosvenor Gallery, and among the well-heeled art gallery attendees are famous artists and writers: the artist James McNeill Whistler and the author and critic Henry James are both present. But they're not whom everyone keeps staring at, nor whom they're talking about. That would be a very tall young man of twenty-three with a round face; longish, wavy hair; and an outlandish coat in a fabric that shines bronze from some angles and red from others. The back of the coat is shaped like a cello. Oscar Wilde, as the man is named, is telling his captivated listeners, "I saw this coat in a dream, worn by a ghost; it looked just like a violoncello. And so I had one made!"

These days, Oscar Wilde is remembered as the prototypical dandy, a glamorous man devoted to style. But Wilde was so much more than that; a prolific and talented writer, thinker, and wit, he also became an accidental martyr for gay rights after his lifestyle—which he lived without shame at a time when being openly homosexual was illegal—sent him to prison and led to his premature death.

ENGLISH FAME, IRISH HEART

THOUGH WILDE FOUND fame in London, he was Irish through and through. He was born and raised in Dublin, where both his parents were prominent intellectuals; his father was a well-known ear and eye surgeon, while his mother was a poet. Wilde was educated at home until he was nine and, after that, sent away to board at Portora, a school intended to prepare him for prestigious Trinity College in Dublin. At Portora, the Oscar Wilde we remember today began to emerge. He excelled at reading and writing and began to flirt with fashion; he wore scarlet and lilac shirts, choosing vibrant colors over plainer choices, and wore his hair long, with a silk hat on top (an unusual choice for a schoolboy on a weekday). He was also openly disdainful of sports, despite his large physical size.

Wilde won a scholarship to Trinity College at age seventeen, where he did well, and by age twenty, he was admitted to study at the even-more-exclusive Oxford. He referred to Oxford as the most "flower-like time" of his life. It was where he truly began to bloom.

At Oxford, Wilde was a social butterfly, known for his wit and

Wilde striking a dramatic pose in a velvet jacket for a publicity photo on his trip to America.

charm as well as his snappy outfits, often formal suits. He told a friend, "If I were all alone marooned on a desert island and had my things with me, I should dress for dinner every evening." He continued to avoid sports and pursued the arts—he wrote poems and managed to get one of them published. As for his home, he decorated his apartment in all white, filled it with lilies and blue china, and had lavish parties for his friends (most of whom were male, though Wilde was not romantically involved with men yet). All of this—the scorn for sports, the appreciation of fine dress and beautiful things—made Wilde Oxford's biggest proponent of Aestheticism. "I find it harder and harder every day to live up to my blue china," he reportedly said.

Though he was famous (or perhaps infamous) at Oxford, Wilde had his real social debut at the Grosvenor Gallery opening in London, when he was taking an unapproved break from school (he was later kicked out for a semester for this extended period of playing hooky). He charmed the gallery crowd with his witty observations, and the way his sharp thinking on art and culture brought him popularity at the party convinced him to "take up the critic's life."

By 1878, Wilde had graduated with a degree in Classics from Oxford, and he was free to do just that.

AESTHETICISM

The Aesthetic movement, which became popular in the late nineteenth century, championed beauty as the most important thing in the fine arts, over deeper political or social themes. In other words, art—literature, music, painting, and so on—didn't need to serve any other purpose than to be beautiful. One phrase that has been used to sum it up is "art for art's sake."

MAKING IT IN AMERICA

BY 1878, WILDE was living in London, socializing with actresses, and writing plays and poetry. He eventually published a book of poetry in 1881. Good though the poems were, they were treated harshly by critics and were so disliked by his housemate's father—he said the poems had an "evil tendency"—that he was kicked out. Unfortunately, his housemate's father owned the house.

The drama did nothing to curb Wilde's ambitions, however, and that same year he was presented with a life-changing opportunity: a speaking tour of America—fifty engagements on the topic of Aestheticism. Wilde seized upon it.

Of course, the first thing on Wilde's agenda was putting together an outfit. Before he departed London, he had a tailor make him a green overcoat, which hung down to his feet, with a fur-trimmed collar and cuffs. He paired it with a smoking cap, a shirt with a "Lord Byron" collar, a blue necktie, and shiny patent leather shoes. With his outfit sorted, he boarded the SS *Arizona*, a ship bound for America, on December 24, 1881. He arrived in New York in early January; when the customs agent asked him what he had to declare, he was rumored to have responded, "I have nothing to declare except my genius."

In England, Wilde had ambition and talent, but he hadn't really made it. But in America, he became a celebrity. His showy fashion choices, including his fur-trimmed green coat and his knee breeches, caused a stir, and local audiences were willing to accept him as an expert on the topic of aesthetics. Journalists hung on his words and printed his witty quotes in newspapers, and the news made it back to Britain. Finally, Wilde was famous.

The tour also made him some money. He used it to travel to Paris,

Another American publicity shot of Wilde.

A MAN STANDS alone on the stage of the sold-out New York City concert hall. The packed audience stares at him in shock and amazement. He is wearing a surprising outfit: a purple sack coat with lace frills at the wrist, knee breeches and silk stockings, and shoes with shiny buckles. Over his shoulders cascades a cloak, and his hair hangs in long waves. Confidently, he addresses the crowd: "We spend our days looking for the secret of life. Well, the secret of life is art."

where he holed up in a hotel and worked on his play *The Duchess of Padua*. Ever the lover of getting into character, he dressed up like the French author Balzac, who was famous for the dressing gown he wore while writing. And so Wilde donned his "writing costume," a white wool dressing gown, which he paired with an ivory cane with a turquoise-covered head. Out on the street, Wilde dressed as stylish Frenchmen did at the time: silk hat, coat, and cuffs turned up. When a friend razzed him about abandoning the style he'd been wearing for years, Wilde said, "All that belonged to the Oscar of the first period. We are now concerned with the Oscar Wilde of the second period, who has nothing whatever in common with the gentleman who wore long hair and carried a sunflower down Piccadilly."

This new Wilde eventually made

his way back to London, where he married an Irish woman named Constance. The wedding gave Wilde an instant respectability that he had lacked before; the morals of a married man's writing were less likely to fall into question. A weekly magazine called *The Bat* thought his transformation was notable enough to write about: "At last he went and cut his hair. . . . He's settled down and married!"

Sedate Wilde didn't last for very long, though. About two years after the wedding, when the couple had had their second child, Wilde began to socialize more heavily with young men again, as he had at Oxford, and stay in hotels (he told Constance this was to concentrate on writing). And then, in 1886 at Oxford, he met a young man named Robert Ross. Ross was a fan of Wilde's poetry and had been beaten up for reading it; he also, according to Wilde, had a "face like Puck," referring to the mischievous elf in Shakespeare's play *A Midsummer Night's Dream*. Ross tried to seduce Wilde—and succeeded.

The two remained friends until the end of Wilde's life.

Discovering he was gay changed Wilde. It deepened his writing, for one: during this time, he wrote his most famous work, *The Picture of Dorian Gray*, one of the first English novels featuring homosexual themes.

Wilde trying to be a family man with Constance and one of their children.

But although Wilde was happy and fulfilled and producing great work, he was also in danger.

In the late nineteenth century, it wasn't technically illegal to be gay in Britain, but it was illegal to have sex with someone of the same gender. Anal sex had been illegal since 1533, and until 1861, it was punishable by death. (Heterosexual couples were almost never charged with this, so it was a law aimed at gay men.) That year, the punishment was lowered to life imprisonment. However, in 1885—just a year before Wilde had his first gay sexual experience—a new law was added that criminalized "gross indecency." It was so vaguely worded that it covered any sort of homosexual behavior; it wasn't necessary to prove that sex ever happened. The punishment was up to two years of hard labor in prison.

Wilde would have known all this, but he probably wasn't too worried. Generally speaking, if you didn't flaunt your homosexuality, English society left you alone. Wilde made excuses

OUTSIDE THE COURTHOUSE, two men grasp a newspaper, staring at its front page. "Look at that absurd suit!" the first man says, pointing at one of the illustrations, which shows a man sitting in a courthouse with long hair, a tidy suit, and an imperious expression.

"Aye, Wilde'll rot in prison," says the other man, pointing at another illustration, showing a man in a prison cell. "The new trial starts this week!"

The men stare up at the courthouse, their anticipation obvious.

to Constance but kept his marriage intact on paper, and he continued his affairs in secret. He probably also felt protected by his skyrocketing fame. His play *Lady Windermere's Fan* was wildly popular, and at its debut he set society atwitter by giving an egotistical, irony-laden speech to the audience while wearing a green carnation in his buttonhole and mauve gloves, holding a cigarette between his fingers.

FORBIDDEN LOVE

BUT IN 1892, something dramatic happened: Wilde fell in love with a young man named Sir Alfred Douglas (who was known by his friends as "Bosie"). The two had an extremely passionate love affair, but Bosie also encouraged Wilde into socially riskier behaviors, such as sex with male prostitutes. Bosie's father, the Marquess of Queensberry—a Scottish nobleman—caught wind of their affair, and to say he was against it is an understatement. In 1894, a book was published called *The Green Carnation*, which depicted Wilde and Bosie's love affair. It attracted Queensberry's ire, though he wasn't yet sure how to focus his anger. But in 1895, when Wilde's play *The Importance of Being Earnest* debuted, Queensberry came up with an idea—to attend the play and pelt rotten vegetables at Wilde. Wilde got wind of the attack and blocked him from entering. But that just made Queensberry even angrier, and he sent a note to Wilde's hotel calling him a "posing sodomite" ("sodomite" was a derogatory word for a man who

Wilde and Bosie.

slept with other men). Wilde was so incensed that he took him to court for libel. And that's where things took a turn. As a defense against the libel claim, Wilde was accused of having relations not just with Bosie but with other men, too. The result was that Wilde himself was charged—with gross indecency. He could have fled to another country to escape, but he didn't. "I decided it was nobler and more beautiful to stay," he said. After a hung jury at his second trial, his third trial resulted in a guilty verdict. He was sentenced to two years of hard labor.

Gentle, social, beauty-loving Wilde was not made for prison. The two years were hard on him. Dressed in a drab prison suit with arrows printed

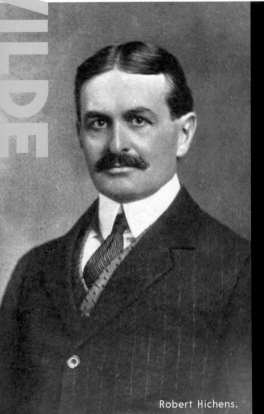

Robert Hichens.

THE GREEN CARNATION

The Green Carnation was written by the satirist Robert Hichens—a gay man and a friend of Wilde's—and published anonymously. The two main characters were clearly based on Wilde and Bosie, and the book depicted their homosexual romance. The *Guardian* review said of it, "*The Green Carnation* will be read and discussed by everyone . . . nothing so impudent, so bold, or so delicious has been printed these many years." Unfortunately for Wilde, the book made him an even more controversial public figure than he had already been.

all over it (meaning it—and by extension, he—was government property), with his hair cut short, Wilde slept on a plank bed, was denied social contact, and was frequently sick. The only bright moment was when, finally, he was allowed to write. While in prison, he wrote one of his great masterpieces, *De Profundis*, which took the form of a long letter to his lover.

After he was released from prison in 1897, Wilde spent the last three years of his life in exile, mostly in France. Destitute—he had gone bankrupt during his trials—he spent his final days in Paris, lonely, disheveled, missing some of his teeth, and begging any acquaintances he came across for money. He fell ill late in 1900 (some say it was late-stage syphilis, but others say it was an ear infection) and died on November 30. He was originally buried outside Paris in the Cimetière de Bagneux, but in 1909, his remains were moved to the Père Lachaise cemetery, within the city. Today, his tomb is encased in a glass barrier to protect it from Wilde's

WILDE'S APHORISMS

Wilde was known for his witty sayings—he published so many that it's impossible to include them all, but these are a few:

"Fashion is a form of ugliness so intolerable that we have to alter it every six months."

"We are all in the gutter, but some of us are looking at the stars."

"I can resist everything except for temptation."

"There is only one thing in the world worse than being talked about, and that is not being talked about."

"To love oneself is the beginning of a lifelong romance."

"To live is the rarest thing in the world. Most people exist, that is all."

Wilde's tomb behind its glass barrier, covered in notes from admirers.

legions of admirers, who were leaving too many lipstick kisses all over the stone.

That Wilde's grave is a tourist attraction is a sign of his lasting legacy. His wit remains legendary (his aphorisms are quoted, and misquoted, all over the place), and his books are still adored. As for his fashion influence, one only needs to look as far as edgy British design house Alexander McQueen, whose Fall 2017 collection was inspired by Wilde. A man who was unjustly imprisoned for loving another man, he has been a gay icon for over a century. At a recent exhibition at the Fashion Institute of Technology called "A Queer History of Fashion: From the Closet to the Catwalk," Wilde's portrait was the first thing visitors saw when they walked in. And rightly so: his life, embodied by his flamboyant fashion choices, is still inspirational today. ◆

TODAY'S DANDIES

Though the term "dandy" was out of fashion by Wilde's time (he preferred "aesthete"), the word has endured—as has the style. Wilde's twenty-first century heirs, modern dandies, still dress their best no matter what.

Clockwise from left: Russell Brand, Pharrell Williams, Harry Styles, André 3000.

FASHION SPOTLIGHT

BEAU BRUMMELL

FULL NAME: George Bryan Brummell

BORN: June 7, 1778, London, England

DIED: March 30, 1840, Caen, France

OCCUPATION: Socialite

BAD BOY CRED: "Beau" Brummell used his talent for dressing well to cross class boundaries—and sparked a fashion craze on the way.

BEFORE WILDE AND his aestheticism brought beauty to men's fashion, social climber Beau Brummell established a new sartorial subculture: dandyism.

Brummell was born middle-class, but his aspirations went far beyond that: he wanted to be a gentleman. He was educated at prestigious schools attended by the upper classes (Eton and Oxford), and after his education, he joined the military and became part of the personal regiment of the Prince of Wales, the heir to the British throne. This proximity allowed him to infiltrate the aristocratic social circles that surrounded the prince.

Brummell's tactic for securing his position among the upper classes was to impress them with his style—an uncommon strategy at a time when class was something you were born into. Rather than simply wearing what other men of his era wore, Brummell took inspiration from his military uniform, hiring military tailors to custom-make clothing for him. Brummell wore slim, cream-colored, full-length trousers with a leather strap over the foot that ensured the fabric stretched over his entire leg, paired with starched shirts with high collars and a tailcoat. Around his neck, he wore a knotted muslin scarf. Supposedly, it took him five hours each day to dress. But his fastidious costuming was worth it when he made dramatic entrances and exits at high-profile social events, ensuring his outfits were noticed.

Before Brummell, fashionable young men in England dressed entirely differently: their clothes were showy and flamboyant, involving lace, knee breeches and stockings, and powdered wigs. The men who dressed this way were called "macaronis"—because the look was considered to be from Continental Europe, like the Italian pasta.

An illustration of Brummell in a typical ensemble.

A closeup of Brummell and his cravat.

known as "dandies." One of Brummell's greatest admirers and imitators was the Prince of Wales himself, who later became King George IV. Despite his widespread influence, Brummell maintained an ironic detachment when discussing his wardrobe, and when asked how he kept his shoes polished to such a shine, he drolly claimed that he used champagne.

Eventually, Brummell's middle-class status caught up with him. He posed as an aristocrat, but he didn't have the funds to continue to dress like one. In his last years, his spending landed him in a debtors' prison, and he died completely broke, and insane from syphilis. Despite his humiliating end, Brummell's influence on fashion was profound: after him, a polished suit became the mark of a well-dressed man, and every generation since has had some version of dandies who know the importance of dressing well. ◆

But Brummell's mode of dress caught on, and the men who, like Brummell, spent their time and money on perfecting tailored wardrobes became

ICONIC LOOK
DONALD GLOVER

Donald Glover is a multitalented actor, Emmy-winning television producer, and Grammy-winning rapper (he performs under the name Childish Gambino), but he's also known for another thing: his style. Most men these days wear pretty much the same thing to formal events: black or dark-blue suits, all different shades of conservative. Glover's smartly tailored, brightly colored suits in luxurious fabrics make him stand out from the crowd.

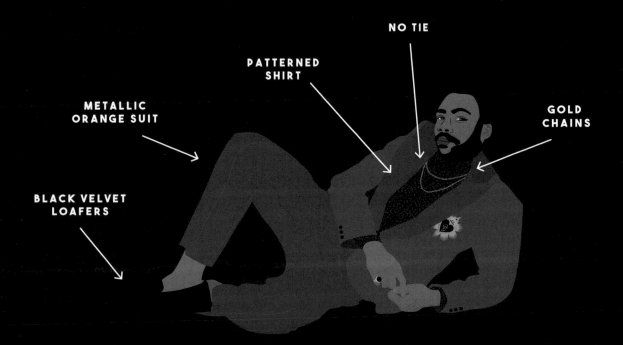

NO TIE

PATTERNED SHIRT

METALLIC ORANGE SUIT

GOLD CHAINS

BLACK VELVET LOAFERS

CHAPTER THREE

MARLON BRANDO

FASHION MACHO

FULL NAME: Marlon Brando Jr.

BORN: April 3, 1924, Omaha, Nebraska

DIED: July 1, 2004, Los Angeles, California

OCCUPATION: Actor, activist

BAD BOY CRED: Brando's emotive performances forever defined rebels as complex characters—clad in leather and denim

MARLON BRANDO

The light of the film projector flickers over the movie theater, revealing a packed house of filmgoers—men wearing buttoned shirts with collars, blazers, and black square-framed glasses, and women in demure dresses with flared skirts, legs neatly crossed. They gaze up at the screen, rapt, slowly lifting popcorn and bottles of soda pop to their mouths in the reflected black-and-white glow of the movie. The man they're watching on screen prowls around with the grace of a cat, wearing tight white T-shirts and undershirts that reveal his youthful, muscled physique. He bursts with energy and emotion, scowling, yelling, and laughing—the crowd can't stop staring, because they're not used to movie stars acting so real. At the film's climax, they gasp as he runs outside, T-shirt ripped, and wails at the top of his lungs: "Stellllaaaaa!"

Ask any film critic and they'll tell you that acting can be divided into two eras: before Brando and after Brando. Over his career, the famous method actor changed acting from something formal and deliberate to something more spontaneous and real. His rule-breaking, defiant attitude extended to the way he dressed, too—and his trademark ensemble of T-shirts, blue jeans, and leather jackets defined the way stylish rebels dressed from the 1950s to today.

YOUNG BUD

BRANDO WAS BORN and raised in the Midwest, growing up with two older sisters in a middle-class family. As a kid, Brando's nickname was Bud. Brando's father was a traveling salesman, and his mother, Dodie, was a creative misfit, an actress who wanted to live an unconventional lifestyle. Dodie was also an alcoholic, and by the time he was a teenager, Brando regularly had to go pick her up from the drunk tank. Brando's father was hardly a model parent, either: he was a serial adulterer who, when he wasn't on the road, was emotionally distant with his children. Without anyone to really look up to, young Bud began strutting around the house like he owned the place—and acquired a lifelong disrespect for authority.

At school, Brando took to befriending kids who didn't fit in. When people were bullied for being different, Brando took them under his wing. Meanwhile, he did everything he could not to blend in: he joined the drama club, started a band, and dressed in jeans paired with brightly colored T-shirts, while most of his classmates wore more conservative attire. He didn't perform well academically and antagonized his school's administration by acting out and playing pranks—in one notorious example, he sprayed the word "SHIT" on the blackboard with lighter fluid and set it on fire.

Brando's behavior got so bad that when he turned seventeen, his parents decided to send him to Shattuck, a military school. But wearing a uniform did little to dispel Brando's mistrust of authority—in fact, it may have made him even more rebellious—and his stay at the school was marked by continuing pranks. Eventually, he intentionally flunked out of the school by informing his commander that in battle, he'd rather flee than take charge of his troop.

MARLON BRANDO

JEANS

Denim clothing has been popular as workwear for hundreds of years, but "jeans," as we know them today, were invented in 1873 by Levi Strauss. The original jeans were tough denim trousers reinforced with metal rivets, and they were worn by manual laborers like factory workers, farmers, cowboys, and miners.

After Brando spent a few months skulking around the family house, his father finally relented and let him attend the sort of school he was truly interested in: theater school.

In 1943, Brando enrolled at the New School in New York. There, he met a woman named Stella Adler, an acting teacher from a Jewish American acting dynasty. Adler was initially wary of Brando due to his rough appearance; he noticed how well the other students dressed, and to communicate his complete lack of interest in fitting in, he would come to class in worn jeans, dirty T-shirts, and beat-up shoes. On the first day of class, Adler took one look at him and asked, "Who's the vagabond?" But, in the end, Brando became her favorite student. Adler taught a new acting strategy—later classified under what is now called method acting—that called for actors to immerse themselves in their roles and try to become the characters by learning more about their values and lives. An example might be that an actor playing a boxer would go to a boxing ring and learn how to box so they could better imagine their character's experiences. Adler also told her students, "Don't be boring." Brando took those words to heart.

THE REALIST

SOON, BRANDO WAS being cast in Broadway plays in New York, and his acting style captivated audiences. While other actors of the 1930s and '40s were professional, deliberate, and predictable, Brando was surprising, unpredictable, and real. He delivered his lines differently every time he acted them out, and because he refused to memorize his lines, he paused in his speeches as if searching for words, like people do in real life. Eventually, he was cast in a play by the famous playwright Tennessee Williams called *A Streetcar Named Desire*, about the downfall of a Southern belle named Blanche DuBois. Brando played a supporting character, a laborer named Stanley Kowalski who was married to Blanche's sister, Stella, but his performance was so electrifying that even though he wasn't the lead, Stanley became the audience's focus.

Despite his newfound success, Brando had no desire to live any sort

Brando dressed in leather in *The Wild One*.

of respectable life. He wore T-shirts, leather jackets, and jeans as a sort of uniform—even to more formal engagements, like premieres and parties—and on the weekends, he let his stubble grow out. His sex appeal was undeniable, and he'd career around the city on his motorcycle with his many dates.

After playing Stanley for a year and a half, Brando began acting in movies. His first was a drama called *The Men*, in which he played a paraplegic World War II veteran. Famously, he researched the role by checking into a veterans' hospital and undergoing physical therapy with a group of real paraplegics—a depth of research that was uncommon for actors at the time. But the film that made him a star was the 1951 movie adaptation of *Streetcar*, in which he again played his role as the virile and irascible Stanley Kowalski. In the film, Brando wore a wardrobe of jeans, white undershirts, and tight T-shirts that revealed his muscular physique. His anguished call to his wife—"Stellaaaaa!"—is one of film's most-quoted lines. The film was a hit and caused a spike in T-shirt sales— due to Brando's on-screen wardrobe,

T-SHIRTS

In the early twentieth century, T-shirts were issued by the Navy and Army as undergarments. Farm workers and laborers integrated them into their work attire, and post–World War II, some veterans began to wear them as casual clothing. But it wasn't until the film version of *A Streetcar Named Desire* that they truly became accepted as everyday wear.

ON SET, THE young man smolders at the camera; he wears a short-sleeved button-up shirt with the sleeves rolled up, and he's all attitude. Another man, slightly older, wearing a T-shirt, jeans, and a leather jacket, takes in the scene, then turns on his heel and leaves. Before he can get out the door, a reporter grabs his arm and asks, "What do you think about James Dean, Mr. Brando?" Brando responds curtly: "Mr. Dean appears to be wearing my last year's wardrobe and using my last year's talent."

Brando clad in his scene-stealing tight T-shirt in *A Streetcar Named Desire.*

men realized T-shirts could be worn as outerwear, not just underwear like they were used to.

Streetcar, whether Brando liked it or not, turned him into a movie idol. The film raked in accolades; it was nominated for eight Academy Awards and won three. But Brando, feigning indifference, skipped the ceremony. He might have been a star, but he was too cool for a stodgy awards ceremony.

In 1953, Brando signed on to film a movie that seemed like a perfect match for his personal style. Titled *The Wild One*, it was about a youth motorcycle gang that invades a small California town. Brando played the leader of the gang, who, in response to the question "What're you rebelling against, Johnny?" famously uttered, "Whaddaya got?" In the film, he wore an outfit not unlike what he wore in real life: leather boots, rolled-up jeans, a white T-shirt, a Perfecto leather jacket, a biker cap, and sideburns. The movie wasn't very good, but it gained a cult following, and Brando's look was widely mimicked: protective clothing that had previously been worn on the back of motorcycles became everyday wear for young rebels. Brando was a style icon for greasers, who emulated his tough-guy look, as well as an inspiration for the "King of Rock and Roll," singer Elvis Presley, who modeled his look in the movie *Jailhouse Rock* after Brando's character in *The Wild One*. He was also a role model for a younger actor named James Dean, who met Brando at Hollywood parties and mimicked both his style and his attitude, to Brando's irritation.

GREASERS

In postwar America in the late 1940s and '50s, youth subcultures flourished. One of these was the "greasers," a working-class subculture defined by their wardrobe of leather jackets, T-shirts, jeans, and the greased-back hairstyle that gave them their name. Because of their lower-class origins, greasers had a reputation of being tough and were often portrayed as the "bad boys" in popular culture, including the movie *Grease*, in which John Travolta plays a greaser from the wrong side of the tracks, and the novel *The Outsiders*, which features battles between greasers and the upper-class Socs.

Brando's comeback as Don Corleone in *The Godfather*.

REBEL WITH A CAUSE

BRANDO'S NEXT FILM, *On the Waterfront*, was a critical success. But by the late 1950s and into the '60s, Brando entered a period of decline. He made a series of critical and commercial flops, and the press trashed him— including the famously acerbic journalist Truman Capote, who published an embarrassingly revealing profile of Brando in the *New Yorker* in 1957 that ruined his aura of mystique and made him seem flawed and deluded. By 1963, movie executives thought of him as box-office poison. But Brando, still a champion of the underdog, had become more interested in activism

Brando marching with James Baldwin and Charlton Heston at the Civil Rights March on Washington, D.C.

than movies, anyway. He supported Martin Luther King Jr. and the civil rights movement and participated in protest actions with the American Indian Movement. He didn't care that he had lost the respect of filmgoing audiences, and began to binge on food (he was known to eat two roast chickens in a single sitting) and put on large amounts of weight.

Just when Brando had hit rock bottom, he was pulled back up by a film called *The Godfather*, in 1972. In it, Brando starred as Vito Corleone, a mafia don. That same year, he appeared in a sexually charged, semi-biographical film called *Last Tango in Paris*, in which he played a forty-eight-year-old man who has a seedy affair with a younger woman. The sex scenes in the film remain notorious to this day—and Brando's co-star later said she felt violated by the way one scene was filmed—but at the time, they reaffirmed that, though he was aging, Brando was still vital. (He was in real life, too, having steamy affairs with both women and men, possibly including the actor Richard Pryor.) The following year, Brando caused more controversy when he skipped the Academy Awards ceremony and sent an Indigenous actress, Sacheen Littlefeather, in his stead, to turn down his Best Actor award in protest of the stereotypical, negative depiction of Indigenous peoples in film.

In his later years, Brando was famous for being a recluse. He hung around with other high-profile celebrities, like Jack Nicholson and Michael Jackson, but mostly remained within his Hollywood compound, eating compulsively, wearing a caftan, until he passed away at age eighty.

Brando's legacy is immense. The way he lived and breathed his performances inspired nearly every serious male actor who came after him, including people such as Jack Nicholson, Daniel Day-Lewis, Joaquin Phoenix, Shia LaBeouf, and David Oyelowo. His moody beauty and on-screen emotional vulnerability set a new standard for male sex symbols, too. No longer did they need to be rigid and stoic to be masculine— Brando showed that a man could be complicated and emotional, too. But his impact on modern style is even more pronounced. Today, T-shirts and jeans are the go-to casual outfit for most men, while men who consider themselves rebels often style those same T-shirts and jeans with leather jackets and boots. The look has changed so little from what Brando wore in the '50s that, if he were transported into the present day, he'd look like any other cool guy on the streets of New York. In the end, Brando never did fit in—he led the way for everyone after him. ◆

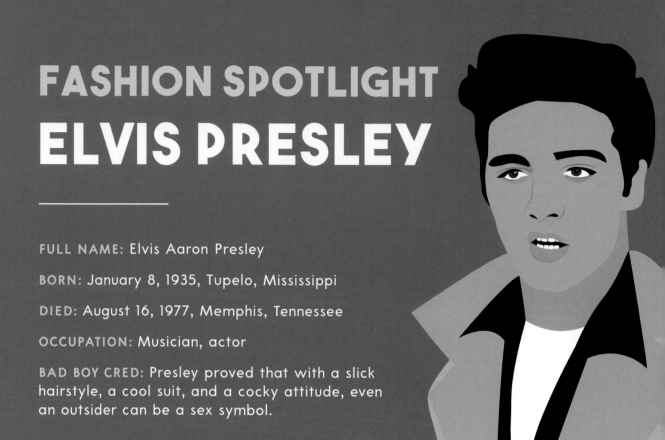

FASHION SPOTLIGHT
ELVIS PRESLEY

FULL NAME: Elvis Aaron Presley

BORN: January 8, 1935, Tupelo, Mississippi

DIED: August 16, 1977, Memphis, Tennessee

OCCUPATION: Musician, actor

BAD BOY CRED: Presley proved that with a slick hairstyle, a cool suit, and a cocky attitude, even an outsider can be a sex symbol.

SWIVELING HIPS, ARTFULLY greased hair, a sharp jacket, and a crowd of screaming girls: Elvis Presley shaped the image of what a rock star should be. And while his style choices might seem predictable today, at the time, Presley was rebelling against society's norms.

Presley was born in a small city called Tupelo and moved with his family at age thirteen to Memphis, where they lived in social housing. At school, Presley was a shy outsider—his classmates called him a "squirrel," slang for "misfit." But he had interests outside of school that kept him busy. Memphis was a hotspot for African American soul, blues, and gospel music, and Presley was a regular attendee at late-night gospel nights. Back at his housing complex, he would play guitar for the other residents; he showed equal appreciation for the music of white country-and-western artists and black blues artists. In town, he hung around music shops—but his favorite store had nothing to do with music. It was Lansky's, a clothing store in the black part of town, and the store owners were familiar with Presley's face from the way he would press it against the glass on his regular visits to gaze at their wares.

In his senior year of high school, Presley bought some much-longed-for clothes from Lansky's—a drape suit in pink and black, his favorite colors. While his classmates wore jeans and work boots and cut their hair in crew cuts, Presley wore polished loafers and dress pants, and tied a scarf around his neck like an ascot. He even got a perm for his long hair (thinking it would make him look like movie star Tony Curtis), applied grease to shape it, and grew sideburns. His classmates thought he was weird, but Presley was creating a new self-image. Finally, in 1954, he walked into the offices of Memphis's

Sun Records and paid with his own money to record a song.

Later that year, Presley's songs had made it onto the radio, but his music was controversial. Some white disc jockeys wouldn't play his music because he sounded, to them, like a black artist—the U.S. was still segregated at the time, and so was its culture—while black stations wouldn't play him because he sounded like a "hillbilly," or a white hick. (His style later became known as "rockabilly.") More controversial were his performances: Presley would wear audacious, colorful suits; grease his hair; and dance sensually, swaying his hips in a way that many, in the sexually repressed culture of 1950s America, considered obscene. Famously, the *Ed Sullivan Show* avoided complaints by filming him from the waist up in 1956 (Ed commented that he thought he could see a soda bottle in Presley's trousers). And in 1957, a critic at the *Los Angeles Mirror-News* acidly commented, "What Elvis offers is not basically music but a sex show." But audiences—particularly young women—went crazy for Presley's sexed-up performances, and he became a megastar, eventually earning the nickname "The King of Rock and Roll," or simply "The King." His rock 'n' roll reign led to a secondary career in Hollywood, where he acted in a series of musical films throughout the '60s.

Presley's later years were his flashiest. After his "comeback" to music in 1968, he became a resident performer in Las Vegas, where his wardrobe was dominated by jumpsuits. The most famous was a white bedazzled jumpsuit with a high collar and a cape that he wore for a live-to-TV concert recorded in Hawaii, while other jumpsuits featured plunging necklines that revealed a masculine swath of chest hair and gold medallions. His comeback didn't stick, sadly, and by 1977, he began to fall apart, famously becoming overweight and addicted to prescription drugs. He died from the complications of his lifestyle at age forty-two.

Elvis during his Vegas years, meeting with President Nixon.

Presley set the standard for what a rock star is, but he also proved that men could be sex symbols. He was one of the first male performers to play up his own desirability; he crafted an image as an icon of heterosexual male beauty, with some inspiration from Hollywood. He said, "I've made a study of Marlon Brando. I've made a study of poor Jimmy Dean. I've made a study of myself, and I know why girls, at least the young 'uns, go for us. We're sullen, we're broodin', we're something of a menace." ◆

ICONIC LOOK
JAMES DEAN

History's most famous rebel might be James Dean. The star of *Rebel Without a Cause* took his fashion inspiration from Brando, copying his jeans, his T-shirts, his leather jackets, and his brooding attitude. Unlike Brando, however, Dean died tragically young—at age twenty-four in a car crash. He didn't get to become an old man like Brando, and he never made any style mistakes; instead, he's forever preserved as a troubled young man in a leather jacket.

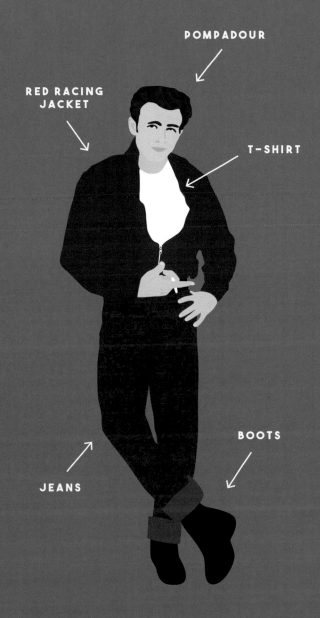

POMPADOUR

RED RACING JACKET

T-SHIRT

BOOTS

JEANS

CHAPTER FOUR

MALCOLM X

FASHION REVOLUTIONARY

FULL NAME: Malcolm Little

BORN: May 19, 1925, Omaha, Nebraska

DIED: February 21, 1965, New York, New York

OCCUPATION: Activist, minister

BAD BOY CRED: Incendiary black rights activist Malcolm X
used fashion to reinforce his revolutionary agenda

MALCOLM X

A black man in a neatly tailored suit, narrow black tie, and black-rimmed glasses stands at a lectern. As he gestures, a ring on his finger bearing a half-moon and a star flashes in the light, while his tailored coat slips up his arm to reveal a black watch. Though he is sedately dressed, his manner is anything but reserved: he is energetic and charismatic, punctuating his emphatic words with the occasional smile.

"Who taught you to hate the texture of your hair?" he asks the African American audience who watch him, rapt. "Who taught you to hate the color of your skin? . . . Who taught you to hate the shape of your nose, and the shape of your lips? Who taught you to hate yourself?"

Malcolm Little, Detroit Red, El-Hajj Malik El-Shabazz: these are all names one man was called throughout his life, but the name he's remembered by is Malcolm X. A fiercely intelligent activist whose trademark black suit and stylish eyeglasses remain iconic today, Malcolm's controversial opinions, charisma, and fearless opposition to racism made him a household name and one of the best-known figures of the American civil rights movement.

COLOR THEORY

A young Malcolm, with his red hair.

MALCOLM WAS BORN in the perfect circumstances to become a black revolutionary. One of eight children of a Baptist minister, the Reverend Earl Little, and a well-educated Grenadian woman named Louise Norton Little, Malcolm became aware early on about racial issues facing African Americans. His father preached to his congregation about the importance of returning to the African homelands of their ancestors—the "Back to Africa" movement. Meanwhile, Malcolm's mother, Louise, led a much different existence because she passed as white. Her black mother had been raped and impregnated by a white man, and Louise was raised without a father— but her appearance was that of a white woman, with pale skin and dark hair. She could avoid the racist attitudes of townsfolk, but only when her husband and children weren't present.

Omaha was a scary place for African Americans in the 1920s, and Malcolm grew up in fear of white supremacist hate groups, like the Ku Klux Klan and the Black Legion, whose anonymous, hooded members rode the countryside on horseback, threatening and assaulting black people, damaging their property, and sometimes killing them. Because of Reverend Little's prominence as

a preacher and the political nature of his sermons, Malcolm's family often received threats—and one day, the threats became a reality. When Malcolm was only six years old, his father was killed; the official ruling was that it was a streetcar accident, but Malcolm's family believed the Reverend had been brutally murdered in the street by the Black Legion. Malcolm's life would never be the same.

After the death of Reverend Little, Malcolm's mother succumbed to stress and financial difficulties and had a mental breakdown; Malcolm and his siblings went into foster care. Malcolm began misbehaving, fighting, and stealing, but being the smart, self-possessed kid that he was, he still got high grades and was elected class president—and expressed interest in becoming a lawyer. But his white teacher told him, "That's no realistic goal for a n——." (At the time, the N-word was used a lot more frequently, sometimes in ignorance but usually to insult black people.) Angered by the exchange, Malcolm began to distrust white people. And at the end of eighth grade, he left school entirely and hopped on a Greyhound bus bound for Boston, where his half sister Ella lived.

Above: The Ku Klux Klan wore white robes and hoods to hide their identities, meaning they could commit racist crimes without personal repercussions.

DETROIT RED

ON A WARM night, a young black man struts by the Apollo Theater. His outfit turns heads: billowing bright-blue pants that cinch at the ankle and a long coat flaring out wildly at the knee. On his head is a blue hat with a feather in the wide brim, barely concealing a shock of red hair. Recognizing him, a musician from the Apollo calls out: "My man! Detroit Red!" He turns and waves. "Hey, daddy-o!" But he doesn't stop—he has somewhere to be.

WHEN MALCOLM ARRIVED in Boston, he knew it was obvious he wasn't a local; people could tell just by the way he dressed. He later described the way he looked as "hick"; that is, an unsophisticated person from the country.

"My kinky, reddish hair was cut hick style, and I didn't even use grease in it. My green suit's coat sleeves stopped above my wrists, the pants legs showed three inches of socks," he said. Much of his first month in the city was spent gawking at the sophisticated African American locals and the polished way they dressed, particularly the hip young black people with their sleek, straightened hair. But it didn't take Malcolm long to adjust. He took a job as a shoeshine boy at a club called the Roseland (most of the nights there were whites-only), where all the cool musicians at the time played. And to erase the embarrassment of his hick past, he reinvented himself with a cool new look: a sky-blue zoot suit with a matching blue hat. The final touch was a "conk," a chemical treatment that made his reddish hair (which he got from his white biological grandfather) straight. Finally, Malcolm was cool.

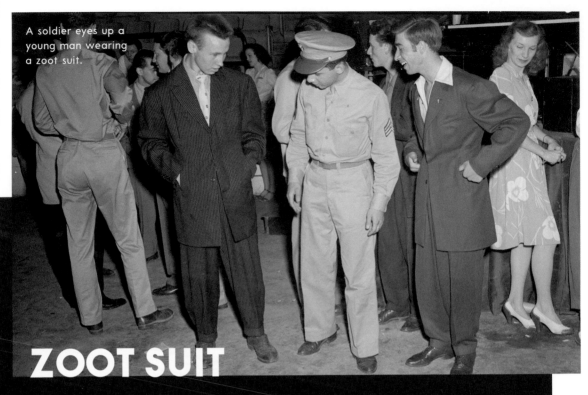

A soldier eyes up a young man wearing a zoot suit.

ZOOT SUIT

A zoot suit is a men's suit with a dramatic outline: it combines trousers that flare widely at the knees and taper at the ankles with a long coat with wide shoulders and broad lapels. The look was popularized by 1940s jazz musicians like Cab Calloway. Zoots became a subcultural fashion statement: wearers were typically rebellious young African American and Latino men. Wearing a zoot identified a man as being cool, edgy, and defiantly anti-mainstream, while it suggested criminality to white authority figures. Zoot suits were also controversial because they required a lot of fabric to manufacture, and wearing them flaunted disregard for wartime rationing. Soldiers serving in World War II were so aggravated by zoot suits that in Los Angeles in 1943, there was a bloody race riot between white military servicemen and Latino zoot suiters.

Malcolm worked the shoeshine job for a while, with some so-called hustles on the side—mostly selling condoms and reefers (marijuana) to club patrons. Eventually, hungry for the energy and culture of the big city, he moved to Harlem, and his main gig became hustling. Because of his job in the club, he knew a lot of musicians, and he sold drugs to them. With his zoots (he bought more after the first) and his stylish look, he fit in with the cool musicians, and he was always able to sell his wares. Around the same time, Malcolm got his street nickname; he was from Michigan, and his hair was red, and so Detroit Red was born. Soon, Malcolm fully and completely transformed into what he later described as a "depraved parasitical hustler." He purchased all his stylish suits stolen—his rationale was that saving money was important, and stolen suits were cheaper. His crimes began to escalate, and he moved on from simply selling drugs to pulling off burglaries.

Eventually, he and his partner in crime involved their white girlfriends in the robberies. Interracial dating happened at the time, but many people disapproved of it, and in some U.S. states, particularly those in the South, interracial marriage was still illegal (and remained so until 1967). Malcolm observed that dating a white woman immediately gave a black man status, while white men were horrified when a white woman dated a black man. Nonetheless, the white women received less scrutiny from people in well-to-do white residential areas, and so they were able to case joints out in the open, and the group pulled off their heists without a hitch. The crime spree only came to an end when Malcolm took a stolen watch in to get fixed and the jeweler recognized the repair. All four of them—the two black men and the two white women—went to court. The women got one to five years in prison; the men got ten years each. Malcolm was only twenty-one. He hadn't yet started shaving.

MALCOLM X

LESSONS BEHIND BARS

PRISON CHANGED MALCOLM, not only because he had to give up his fancy suits to wear a pair of faded dungarees stenciled with his inmate number, but also because it immediately forced him to sober up. When he'd been on the street hustling, he had taken a lot of drugs, and he didn't have access to them in prison. Due to his bad attitude, the other inmates nicknamed him "Satan." But things changed after Malcolm's brother, a little mysteriously, wrote to inform him that he might get out of prison if he stopped consuming pork and smoking cigarettes. He then visited in person and explained to Malcolm that he belonged to an organization called the Nation of Islam and that the white man was "the devil." Malcolm thought back over the times in his life when he had suffered—often, a powerful white man had been the one to deliver that suffering—and decided that his brother had a point.

Malcolm began to write letters to the leader of the Nation of Islam, a man named Elijah Muhammad. To Malcolm's surprise, Muhammad wrote back, and the two men began a lengthy correspondence. Emboldened, Malcolm began writing more letters, including to the president of the United States. Writing these letters inspired Malcolm to seek out an education, and so he began to spend time at the prison library, poring over history books. Two of the most important things he learned were how history had been whitewashed, and how rich and beautiful black history was.

And then, in 1952, after seven years in prison, Malcolm got parole.

Elijah Muhammad, the leader of the Nation of Islam from 1934 to 1975.

THE NATION OF ISLAM

The Nation of Islam (NOI) is a political and religious organization devoted to the advancement of African Americans. Its beliefs are based on the religion of Islam, but most adherents of traditional Islam don't consider the NOI to be a true branch of their faith. It differs from traditional Islam in several ways, including a spiritual belief that black people are the original people on Earth and all white people are "devils" created by a scientist named Yakub on the Greek island of Patmos. While the NOI has done some good with its campaign for black rights, some of its beliefs are extreme; Martin Luther King Jr. referred to it as a "hate group."

A NEW LIFE

WHEN MALCOLM LEFT prison, he was issued what he called a "cheap Li'l Abner suit" (referring to a comic strip about hillbillies). Before he hopped on a bus to Detroit to live with one of his brothers, he purchased three important items: a nice-looking pair of glasses, a wristwatch, and a suitcase. Then he was off.

Soon after he arrived in Detroit, Malcolm joined Detroit Temple Number One, one of the Nation of Islam's places of worship. Malcolm was so dedicated to the organization —after all, the Nation of Islam was what had inspired his transformation from street hustler to scholar—that he was amazed there were empty seats. He quickly took on the role of recruiting new followers, and he also changed his name: no longer was he Malcolm Little, and he certainly wasn't Detroit Red. Now he was Malcolm X. Within the Nation of Islam, adherents would take on a new, Islamic name, and while they were waiting, they used an "X," symbolizing the fact that in America, black people's last names were inherited from former slave masters. Substituting an "X" allowed a person to shed that history and acknowledge the unknown nature of their African heritage.

Malcolm rapidly rose within the Nation of Islam, eventually becoming a minister, marrying someone he considered to be a respectable black woman, and settling down. He became known for his impassioned lectures on racism and reclaiming black power, and his natural charisma made it easy for him to recruit new members. He was instantly recognizable, too: a tall black man in a sharply tailored, single-breasted dark suit and a skinny tie, paired with a wristwatch and a pair of stylish glasses. Gone was the conk; instead, his naturally curly red hair was cropped close. His look, which combined Muslim modesty, pride in his African heritage, and polished style, gave him an air of respectability and intellectualism: precisely what he needed to recruit followers to a religious organization that was rapidly becoming very powerful and very famous.

But more than the Nation of Islam, it was Malcolm himself who was becoming famous, and the Nation of Islam was not happy with his celebrity. His incendiary speeches were constant fodder for the media, and his philosophy, which included racial segregation and equality for blacks "by any means necessary" (presumably including violence), made him infamous. The press called him "hateful," and his methods were negatively compared to the peaceful civil rights activism of Martin Luther King Jr., whose nonviolent methods Malcolm openly criticized: "Concerning nonviolence: it is criminal to teach a man not to defend himself," he said. After one particularly controversial statement to the media in 1963 about the assassination of beloved president John F. Kennedy—Malcolm coldly referred to it as "chickens coming home to roost," meaning that the violence of white society had been the cause—he was suspended. Malcolm publicly split from the Nation of Islam, knowing that this would put him in danger of violent retaliation from members of the organization. He set off to open his own mosque, but felt that in order to do so, he needed to learn more about traditional Islam—and so he made the journey to the Saudi Arabian city of Mecca to do the hajj, a holy pilgrimage that Muslims are encouraged to do at least once in their lives.

In Mecca, Malcolm discovered that not all Muslims looked the same. Some were dark-skinned, like him, and others were what he considered to be white. And to his surprise, everyone treated one another as equals; he didn't feel the same kind of racial tension that he did in America.

The trip changed Malcolm. He officially became a Sunni Muslim and changed his name to El-Hajj Malik El-Shabazz—his "Muslim name." Importantly, he also changed his perspective on race. He realized that it was possible for people from different backgrounds to exist in harmony,

BLACK POWER MOVEMENT

Malcolm X was one of the major inspirations for the Black Power movement, which took off after his death in 1965. The most prominent organization in the movement was the Black Panthers, who called for an armed fight for black power. The Panthers, who coined the phrase "Black is beautiful," had a distinctive and instantly recognizable look: Afros, black berets, dark sunglasses, black leather jackets, black pants, and boots. At the 2016 Super Bowl, Beyoncé's backup dancers dressed in the Panther uniform, and the media interpreted her entire performance as being about black pride.

without racism; white people weren't necessarily devils after all.

After he returned to America, Malcolm returned to public life, preaching his new, softened attitude toward racial diversity, but his relationship with the Nation of Islam grew worse. He regularly received death threats from them, which led to a very famous photo shoot that appeared in *Ebony* magazine in 1964 depicting Malcolm, in a slender silver suit and a narrow black tie, peering through the windows of his apartment while holding a rifle. It was a carefully prepared visual message from Malcolm to the Nation of Islam: he was as smooth and collected as ever, and he was ready to protect his family.

Tragically, Malcolm's posturing did not save him. In 1965, he was giving a speech to a crowd in Manhattan when a man burst out of the crowd and shot Malcolm twenty-one times, killing him. Two Nation of Islam members went to prison for the crime.

When he died, Malcolm's views were still controversial—he never gave up the hard-line attitude of "by any means necessary"—but nonetheless, he was one of the most important and powerful members of the civil rights movement. Today, his image carries the same potent revolutionary energy that it did in the '60s, and his words, image, and style have been a recurring motif in black culture, hip hop in particular. In the video for Public Enemy's 1991 song "Shut 'Em Down," Malcolm's face appears on the American dollar bill, while the rapper T.I. dressed up as him on the cover of *VIBE* magazine in 2009. The notoriously fashionable Kanye West couldn't help name-checking him, too, on his song "Good Morning." If Malcolm had lived, it's hard to say where his philosophy would have led him; his work remains unfinished. But racism is still a destructive force in America and around the world, and as Malcolm X was one of the people who fought against it most fiercely, invoking him—whether on a T-shirt, in song lyrics, or as a style icon—is a righteous claim for black equality. ◆

FASHION SPOTLIGHT
CHE GUEVARA

FULL NAME: Ernesto Guevara de la Serna

BORN: June 14, 1928, Rosario, Argentina

DIED: October 9, 1967, La Higuera, Bolivia

OCCUPATION: Revolutionary leader

BAD BOY CRED: Guevara's guerilla style proclaimed him a warrior for the people and turned him into an icon.

A YOUNG MAN with long hair, a mustache, and a beret with a star on it, gazing rebelliously into the distance: this iconic image of Che Guevara is everywhere. Printed on T-shirts, posters, mugs, and more, it's sometimes claimed to be the most reproduced photo in history. Those who wear Guevara's face on a T-shirt are usually trying to say one simple thing:

"I'm a rebel." Of course, Guevara's history is more complicated than that.

Guevara was born into a middle-class family and was wealthy enough to attend medical school in cosmopolitan Buenos Aires, but his observations of poverty were what defined his life. Most of Guevara's friends were from the lower classes, and he was aware of the difference between his lifestyle and theirs. Intellectual Guevara loved books and poetry, and he pointedly disdained stylish clothes. His main item of clothing was a white shirt that he called "the weekly" (which was how often he cleaned it). He wore old, sometimes mismatched boots, and he most certainly did not wear a tie. But it wasn't just laziness: Guevara loved the attention that his slovenly dress earned him, and relished his nickname: *El Chancho* (the Pig).

Midway through university, Guevara and a friend embarked on a motorcycle tour of South America. The desperate poverty he witnessed convinced him that the only answer was a Marxist (Communist) revolution. In 1953, Guevara finished his degree and, almost immediately after, went to Guatemala, where he witnessed an American-backed coup that overthrew the leftist elected government, further radicalizing him. While he was there, his frequent use of the word *che*, Argentine slang that roughly translates to "bro" or the filler "eh," earned him his legendary nickname.

Soon after, while living in Mexico, Guevara met a pair of Cuban brothers and revolutionaries: Raúl and Fidel Castro. The two were planning to overthrow the right-wing government in Cuba, and Guevara decided he wanted to be involved. The rest is history: Guevara, clad in green military fatigues, black boots, and a black beret—the uniform of a revolutionary—was second in command during the Cuban Revolution, a violent armed revolt that transformed the country into a Communist dictatorship by 1959.

Post-revolution, Guevara took on several roles within the Cuban government, but he refused to adopt the usual political uniform: rather than put on a suit, as most leaders would have done, he remained in his green fatigues. It was a potent symbol: Guevara would never be a tool of the establishment (or so he wanted people to believe). And by 1966, with Communism firmly established in Cuba, Guevara decided to leave to stoke revolution in other countries. He traveled to the

Che in his fatigues and beret.

journalist. First used for propaganda purposes within Cuba, the portrait was soon reproduced as a poster, used in student marches and adopted by the hippie culture of the era: after all, with his long hair and defiant gaze, Guevara had the look of a counter-culture icon (though the violence he engaged in, which victimized many innocent Cubans, was the opposite of peace-loving hippie ideals).

Today, Guevara's image is used relentlessly, sometimes in confusing ways: in 2017, couture brand Chanel's Cruise collection featured images of models in Havana—the capital of still-Communist Cuba, where buildings are dilapidated and poverty is common—clad in high-fashion fatigues and black berets. Expensive clothing that only the richest people can afford is the opposite of what El Chancho really stood for. But Guevara's ideals have been boiled down into a simple concept—rebellion—that doesn't come close to capturing his passionate pursuit of revolution at any cost. ◆

Congo and then to Bolivia, where, in 1967, he was captured and killed by the Bolivian army.

After Guevara's death, his image became a symbol of rebellion and struggle throughout the world, largely owing to one portrait: *Guerrillero Heroico*, taken by the photographer Alberto Korda in 1960. Prior to the revolution, Korda had actually been a fashion photographer, which may have given him more of an eye for style and drama than a typical photo-

ICONIC LOOK
MAO ZEDONG

Originally developed by revolutionary leader Sun Yat-sen as a form of Chinese dress combining Eastern and Western style, the Mao suit was made famous by the founder of the People's Republic of China, Mao Zedong—a man revered by some, but considered by others to be a brutal dictator. The suit became a symbol of the common man during China's Cultural Revolution. It was also popular in the West during the '60s and '70s, when intellectuals sympathetic to Communism would wear it with a turtleneck underneath. Today, it's still a symbol of nationalism in China, and serves as inspiration for men's collections from designers like John Galliano and Vivienne Westwood.

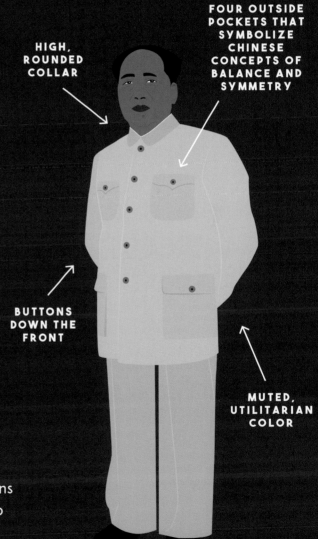

HIGH, ROUNDED COLLAR

FOUR OUTSIDE POCKETS THAT SYMBOLIZE CHINESE CONCEPTS OF BALANCE AND SYMMETRY

BUTTONS DOWN THE FRONT

MUTED, UTILITARIAN COLOR

CHAPTER FIVE

ANDY WARHOL

FASHION ARTIST

FULL NAME: Andrew Warhola

BORN: August 6, 1928, Pittsburgh, Pennsylvania

DIED: February 22, 1987, New York, New York

OCCUPATION: Artist, filmmaker

BAD BOY CRED: Warhol's deft manipulation of consumer culture, celebrity, and his own image set the stage for every eccentric trendsetter who followed him.

ANDY WARHOL

On a sunny afternoon on Madison Avenue, men wearing tailored suits rush down the street, heading back from lunch to their jobs in advertising. But one of these men doesn't look like the others. Wearing a white-blond wig, he walks quickly but delicately, almost like a dancer, wearing thick granny glasses, a suit splattered with paint, and a pair of shoes that look expensive but beaten up. He has a tie knotted around his neck, but he's cut off the fabric where the tie ends didn't line up. Despite his odd appearance, he seems to be recognized by everyone here: "Hey, Andy!" they call as he passes, patting him on the back. "Don't we have a meeting today, Andy Warhol?"

As one of the founders of the pop art movement, Andy Warhol elevated everyday objects to the status of art— his *Campbell's Soup Cans* are among the most famous paintings of the twentieth century. Warhol's reach extended beyond art, too: he was also a commercial artist, filmmaker, book publisher, nightlife promoter, and music producer. But Warhol's greatest work of art may have been himself. Obsessed with celebrity, he carefully maintained an image that, as much as his art, was responsible for making him a star.

DREAMING OF FAME

GROWING UP IN a crowded immigrant ghetto in Pittsburgh as the youngest of three boys in a Hungarian family, Warhol's early life was humble. His father was a workaholic —a trait Warhol inherited—but Warhol's true inspiration came from the women in his life. He clung to his artistic mother, helping her pick out her clothes and hats. All his friends at school were girls, and Warhol modeled his appearance and behavior after them.

His fascination with celebrity first took root at age eight, when he came down with rheumatic fever, which then progressed into a neurological disorder called St. Vitus's Dance. Warhol needed to stay home from school and rest—and in his copious free time, he read movie magazines and daydreamed about Hollywood. The child star Shirley Temple became his idol: he wrote her fan letters and began to imitate her, borrowing her gestures and mannerisms and making them his own.

By high school, Warhol had developed into an odd, quiet boy; he wore his white hair with bangs or swept back, along with a sweater vest, a shirt with rolled-up sleeves, and saddle shoes. Other students teased him about his pale complexion by calling him "the albino." Despite the teasing, Warhol was beginning to show real talent in art. He decided to pursue post-secondary art education at the Carnegie Institute of Technology, where, due to his childlike appearance and naive mannerisms, he was adopted by the other students as the "class baby." By the end of his third year, his skills won him a job in the display department of Pittsburgh's main department store, painting backdrops for window displays. He took the job seriously and, as a sign of his enthusiasm, painted his nails a different color each day. His new paycheck allowed him to purchase his "dream suit": an impractical, showy, cream-colored corduroy number that clearly set him apart as an artist and a man of style. A year later, in 1949, Warhol graduated and moved to the epicenter of both art and style: New York.

Warhol was made for New York. He quickly built up successful relationships with major fashion magazines and advertising firms for commercial illustration. He had a strategy for catching the attention of creative directors: inspired by Marlon Brando's appearance in *A Streetcar Named Desire*, he wore worn-out sneakers, chinos, and a T-shirt, and rather than a briefcase, he carried his work in a paper bag. The whole look, which his friends dubbed "Raggedy Andy," was intended to signal that Warhol needed work, and people bought it. By 1952, he was making $25,000 a year—

TRUMAN CAPOTE

An author and playwright, Truman Capote was a force in New York's social scene in the 1950s. A young, stylish socialite with cultural panache—he wrote both *Breakfast at Tiffany's* and *In Cold Blood*—he quickly became an idol for Warhol, eclipsing Shirley Temple.

roughly $230,000 in today's money. With his newfound wealth, Warhol began to buy nicer clothes—but he wouldn't allow them to stay that way. He'd soak his new leather shoes with water, splatter them with paint, and wear them untied, and when he put on a tie, if the ends didn't meet, he'd take a pair of scissors and cut them off to the same length. Because he was balding, he started wearing a hat and then a toupee. Due to his poor vision, he also bought thick-lensed Coke-bottle glasses. His look was, to say the least, unique.

Warhol's enthusiasm for commercial art was unusual for an artist—advertising was considered a lesser pursuit, and artists usually hated it. Warhol's new idol, Truman Capote, had even belittled his fan by referring to him as a "window-decorator type" (that is, frivolous and probably gay—both of which Warhol was). But real art-world success was something Warhol still yearned for. In 1956, he had his first show at a small co-op gallery; the art mostly depicted penises

IT'S EARLY MORNING in New York, and the party is still going at this midtown Manhattan art studio. From floor to ceiling, everything is silver except for a few pieces of art, which lean against the walls. Everyone in the room is beautiful, well-dressed, and dancing to the loud music. In the corner, a man stands alone, taking in the scene. He wears tight black jeans, a T-shirt, a black leather jacket, and dark sunglasses; on his feet are high-heeled black boots. His silver wig gleams in the low light.

adorned with various things (lipstick, bows, etc.). The sexual and gay themes of the art meant that it didn't sell very well, but a few pieces made it into the collection of the Museum of Modern Art (MoMA), meaning that Warhol had officially crossed over into the "real" art world.

OUTSIDER ART

DESPITE WARHOL'S AMBITIONS, the real art world still wouldn't have him. Partly, this was because he was still thought of as a commercial artist—and partly because he was openly gay. In the 1950s, the psychiatric industry defined homosexuality as a mental illness, and in most states, homosexual acts were illegal. Gay art and literature were often condemned as obscene. The revelation that someone was gay could destroy that person's career, and when Warhol approached other successful gay artists, like Jasper Johns and Robert Rauschenberg, at parties, they snubbed him—they weren't publicly out, and they didn't

ABSTRACT EXPRESSIONISM

Abstract expressionism is an art form that relies on spontaneity, brushstrokes that imply motion, and the lack of a formal shape. Some abstract expressionist works, like those of Jackson Pollock, are composed of a large number of globs of paint; others, like those of Mark Rothko, are large, abstract paint shapes on canvas.

Warhol's famous *Campbell's Soup Cans.*

want to be associated with him. In reaction, Warhol declared that he was "starting" pop art. "Because I hate abstract expressionism. I hate it!"

Warhol wasn't the creator of pop art, but he was the artist who would end up being the most famous for it. He began making large paintings of advertisements, but another artist, Roy Lichtenstein, was painting large-scale comics (another "lesser" art) in a more sensational way, stealing all of Warhol's thunder. Things didn't really

turn around for Warhol until he asked a friend for a suggestion of what he should paint, and she told him, "You should paint something that every-body sees every day, that everybody recognizes . . . like a can of soup."

Warhol proceeded to create a series of thirty-two Campbell's Soup cans—every variety of soup they produced in 1962—painted onto large white canvases. When they were first shown at a gallery in Los Angeles in the summer of 1962, they attracted both attention and controversy for pushing the boundaries of what traditionalists thought art should be. And Warhol's next show, at a gallery in New York, pushed things even further, for he adopted an even less painterly means of production: silk-screening. For this show, he reproduced a number of his earlier works, including his soup cans, as silk screens. He also added a diptych—artwork shown in two panels side by side—of Marilyn Monroe, who had recently died. The show was controversial; many labeled Warhol a fraud. But it was a smash success and almost sold out. It also added to Warhol's mystique. After that, when he appeared at parties, with his white wig and an entourage in tow—usually a bunch of beautiful young women—people would stop and stare. One of his friends at the time claimed he was a polarizing figure because "he looked like pop art."

SILK-SCREENING

Silk-screening (or screen printing) is a printing technique whereby an image can be printed onto another substrate by transferring ink or paint through the mesh of a screen—multiple times. Underground artists used it to print movie posters and flyers, but Warhol was the first to bring it to the mainstream.

FACTORY WORKERS

EVENTUALLY, WARHOL WAS producing so much art that he needed to work out of a studio. In 1963, after six months in one studio, he rented a space in a factory on East 47th Street in Manhattan. At the Factory (which the space was dubbed), an assistant helped him mass-produce large quantities of screen prints, sculptures, and other art pieces. Decorated in all silver, the Factory turned into a hangout for cool, creative, often gay misfits from New York's downtown scene, many of whom were experimenting freely with drugs. Soon, Warhol began to use the place as a film studio; he made avant-garde art films, casting Factory regulars in roles. Some of these people became what he called his "Superstars," favorites whom he would shower with attention, cast in starring roles, and bring with him to public events. The most famous among these was Edie Sedgwick, a beautiful, troubled young heiress with

Warhol in front of a film featuring Sedgwick.

a boyish look and white-blond hair. Warhol saw her as a sort of extension of himself and modeled himself after her, much like he did with his female friends when he was a little boy; when they appeared in public, with Warhol in tight black clothes and a white wig, the two were mirror images. At home, Warhol would wear black tights and a striped shirt in imitation of her. Eventually, however, Warhol tired of Sedgwick and pushed her out of his life to focus his energies on other Superstars.

Experimenting with film was just the beginning of Warhol's transformation from artist into a creative impresario with fingers in many different pies. In late 1965, one of the Factory's hangers-on led Warhol to see a band called The Velvet Underground, a spacey, psychedelic band with songs about drugs and a counterculture vibe. Warhol took a liking to them at first sight and within days arranged to manage the band, setting them up with a glamorous, ethereal German singer named Nico. Warhol booked them to play at a

IN A NIGHTCLUB in Greenwich Village, a band plays psychedelic music. Most of the band is dressed in black, but they're fronted by an angelic woman with long blond hair, dressed all in white. In front of them, a crew of interpretive dancers pretend to flog one another and perform crucifixions. Some people in the audience look horrified; others look amazed. A figure in a striped boatneck shirt, suit jacket, silver wig, and sunglasses watches over the show.

nightclub, accompanied by strobe lights and interpretive dancers. This multimedia spectacle was dubbed the Exploding Plastic Inevitable, and everyone who was anyone in New York wanted to be there.

Warhol had his fans, but he also had his enemies; his aloofness and habit of using people and throwing them away, as he did with Sedgwick, provoked some resentments. That resentment boiled over with the appearance of Valerie Solanas, a radical feminist who attempted to get Warhol to produce her play, *Up Your Ass*, and who appeared in one of Warhol's movies—though she's most famous for writing the *SCUM Manifesto* in 1967, which declared that society could only be fixed by eliminating men. In 1968, she began to call him with threats, and in June of that year, she arrived at the Factory, pulled out a gun, and shot him three times. Warhol didn't die, but a five-hour operation left him with scars and pain that took him years to overcome. Solanas, meanwhile, turned herself in to the authorities, was diagnosed with schizophrenia, and went to prison.

It took Warhol a while to return to normal after his ordeal, but by 1971, he was jet-setting to Europe to produce movies. His attire reflected his new lease on life: now he was a dandy who favored velvet jackets and European designer shirts worn with a tie; in his arms, he carried around a miniature dachshund named Archie. And he had a new vehicle for his celebrity: a magazine called *Interview*.

FIFTEEN MINUTES OF FAME

In 1968, a Swedish museum showed a retrospective of Warhol's work, and the exhibition catalog quoted him as saying, "In the future, everyone will be world-famous for 15 minutes." The quote came to represent the sort of mass-produced, disposable, yet expensive artwork that Warhol produced, as well as the fleeting fame of modern celebrity.

Warhol presenting his presidential portrait to President Jimmy Carter.

When it launched in 1969, *Interview* was a movie magazine but evolved to become a high-end publication that promoted Warhol's own lifestyle. It featured interviews with celebrities and showcased the pursuits of Warhol and his crew of cultural elites. (It still exists to this day, without Warhol's involvement.)

In the '80s, Warhol wasn't anti-establishment anymore; as weird as he was, he *was* the establishment. The feeling at the Factory was that he'd gotten into a tired groove. Things changed, however, when he met an edgy young artist named Jean-Michel Basquiat. Warhol took Basquiat under his wing and let him work at the Factory, and the partnership gave Warhol a youthful new energy; out were the dandyish suits, and in were black leather jackets, black jeans, and sunglasses. Other young artists around him began to refer to him as "The Pope."

By 1987, Warhol was still wildly successful, flying to different cities for art openings where he was as much an attraction as his art. But physically, he wasn't doing so well. He had gallstones but, due to a fear of hospitals, refused to have an operation. Eventually, however, things got so bad that he had to submit himself to surgery—and, sadly, his fears turned out to be justified. Warhol died in his hospital room after his operation from a cardiac arrhythmia. He was buried wearing a suit, paisley tie, platinum wig, and sunglasses.

BEYOND 15 MINUTES

THIRTY YEARS AFTER his death, Andy Warhol is unavoidable. His art is a common motif in fashion, and collections based on his art have appeared on the runways of designers like Stephen Sprouse and Versace. Tom Ford's 2016 collection was inspired by what Warhol wore himself: striped shirts, natty suits, leather jackets, and, of course, sunglasses. Looking at photos of Warhol, his uniqueness is striking. A fashionable weirdo, his look is still as fresh today as it was in the '70s—his obsessive attention to his own image produced the result he was after. While the maxim about fifteen minutes of fame was an eerily accurate prediction about our current, short-lived obsessions with Instagram celebrities and Twitter spats, Warhol's own fame is proof that some things are meant to last. ◆

FASHION SPOTLIGHT
JEAN-MICHEL BASQUIAT

FULL NAME: Jean-Michel Basquiat

BORN: December 22, 1960, New York, New York

DIED: August 12, 1988, New York, New York

OCCUPATION: Artist

BAD BOY CRED: Basquiat's wild style erased the boundaries between street culture and the art world.

"THE RADIANT CHILD"—that's how a fawning *Artforum* profile referred to Jean-Michel Basquiat in 1981. An American artist who transitioned from graffiti writer to art-world darling and died tragically young, Basquiat made brilliant artwork that brought the energy of the streets into the art world.

Basquiat grew up in a middle-class family in Brooklyn; his father, who was born in Haiti, was a successful accountant, while his mother, who was of Puerto Rican descent, was a cultured woman who often took her son to art galleries. A traumatic childhood event helped shape Basquiat's later art career: when he was six years old, he was hit by a car and required an operation to remove his damaged spleen. While he was recovering, his mother gave him a copy of the medical manual *Gray's Anatomy*. The anatomical drawings he studied later became themes in his paintings.

As a teen, Basquiat was troubled; his mother had become mentally ill, his parents separated, and he ran away from home for a while. He began attending an alternative school in Manhattan meant for bright, creative students who were struggling in other environments. He was expelled, however, after he threw a pie at the principal; after the incident, his father kicked him out of the house for good, and he began staying with friends in Manhattan. The artistically inclined seventeen-year-old was simultaneously fascinated and repelled by New York's art scene, and he teamed up with a friend to write graffiti in Manhattan, mostly around SoHo, where art galleries were located. Tagging (that is, writing his name on walls) under the name SAMO, which was pronounced "same-oh" and stood for "same old shit," Basquiat created tags—all including a copyright symbol—that were witty, provocative, and aimed at art-world elites. One, for example, proclaimed, "SAMO FOR THE ART PIMPS."

Another said, "SAMO AS A RESULT OF OVEREXPOSURE."

But Basquiat wanted into the very world he mocked. He cultivated a distinctive appearance that made him easily recognized around Manhattan: initially, he had a bleach-blond Mohawk and, later, dreadlocks that he tied into pigtails, which he wore with thrift-shop clothes. He began to make art: drawings on matchbooks and small photocopied "baseball cards." He made his first entrée to the art world by boldly approaching Warhol at a restaurant and selling him a baseball card.

Soon, Basquiat began to paint larger works, about which he claimed, "I want

Basquiat's painting *Boy and Dog in a Johnnypump.*

to make paintings that look as if they were made by a child." Wildly emotive, they featured scrawled figures, copyright symbols, human figures, crowns, and words. One of the sources Basquiat cited was voodoo, while some critics saw a tie to Cy Twombly, whose art featured large, looping words. The paintings were a success, and soon, Basquiat was a massive star, raking in huge amounts of money from his paintings, palling around with Warhol, and dating a pre-fame Madonna. Famously, he worked in Armani suits, recklessly splattering them with paint. Now that he had money, he became obsessed with fashion and even modeled in a Comme des Garçons fashion show. Nice clothes were a way for him to claim legitimacy to those who wanted to pigeonhole him as a black artist working in a predominantly white art world. "I am not a black artist, I am an artist," he proclaimed. Despite his stylish clothes, however, Basquiat suffered discrimination, both in the art world and on the street; even as a millionaire artist dressed in designer clothes, he had difficulties catching a cab at night.

Sadly, the pressures of fame and wealth got to Basquiat. He developed a notorious hard drug habit, reportedly dropping up to $30,000 in one go on heroin. He lost his battle with addiction at only age twenty-seven, when he died from an overdose.

Basquiat's tragic demise only increased the value of his paintings. Today, a single Basquiat is worth millions; his most expensive painting sold for $110.5 million in 2017, making it the most expensive artwork produced by an American artist. His singular talent has made him an inspiration to many; it's easy to see his influence on artists like José Parlá and Oscar Murillo as well as the aesthetics of young men today. Jay-Z paid homage to Basquiat one Halloween by dressing up like him, while The Weeknd, with his dreadlocked pigtails and designer clothes, has clearly adopted Basquiat as a fashion muse. In the thirty years since his death, Basquiat's influence hasn't faded away. ◆

ICONIC LOOK
TAKASHI MURAKAMI

Takashi Murakami is the founder of the postmodern art movement called "Superflat," inspired by Japanese manga (comics), a so-called low art form that Murakami has elevated to high art. Murakami has collaborated with many fashion designers, most notably Louis Vuitton. At public events, he knows how to make an entrance: he has dressed as an octopus, a jellyfish, and a catlike robot named Mr. DOB—all characters that defy the seriousness of the art world and communicate his dedication to being superflat.

OCTOPUS HAT

ROUND GLASSES

LONG HAIR

TENTACLE JACKET

SILVER SNEAKERS

CHAPTER SIX

KARL LAGERFELD

FASHION CHARACTER

FULL NAME: Karl Otto Lagerfeld

BORN: September 10, 1933, Hamburg, Germany

OCCUPATION: Fashion designer

BAD BOY CRED: Lagerfeld styled himself as an aristocrat and became fashion royalty.

KARL LAGERFELD

Tanned, supple bodies line the pool overlooking the Seine River at the Piscine Deligny. All the cool young people of Paris are here to see and be seen, and they chatter, suntan, and occasionally strut in front of the crowd to jump in the water. But heads turn when one man in particular sashays past. He's wearing a one-piece, strappy swimsuit that dips low in the front, while all the other men at the pool wear simple trunks. On his feet are a pair of high heels, and his black hair is swept back into perfect position. "My god," one woman whispers to her friend. "Who is that?" "Oh," her friend replies, "that's Karl Lagerfeld. I hear he's a massively wealthy German aristocrat. No wonder he's such a show-off."

With the white ponytail, black sunglasses, and black fingerless gloves he sports today, Karl Lagerfeld is one of the most recognizable figures in fashion. But he didn't become "Kaiser Karl," the so-called Pope of Fashion, by coasting on an aristocratic legacy, as some might think. No: Lagerfeld got where he is today by creating a character.

ECCENTRIC YOUTH

WEALTH AND A noble lineage are things Lagerfeld likes to make claims to, but in truth, he was born in Hamburg to middle-class parents. His father worked in a managerial role at a milk company, and the family certainly did well, but they didn't own castles or carry royal blood. When Lagerfeld was one year old, his father moved the family to Bad Bramstedt, a small town in a rural area outside of Hamburg. That's where Lagerfeld grew up, in a nice four-bedroom house on a wooded piece of land.

Lagerfeld's interest in fashion began early; by age three, he would admire pictures of women in nice clothing in magazines and cut them out. As he grew older, he grew more eccentric. He played with dolls at home and hated sports, and his habits, unusual for boys at the time, made him unpopular at school. His classmates considered him girly, and he didn't really have many friends. And then there was his style: while everyone else was casual, Lagerfeld was particular about his look and always dressed up in a jacket, tie, and long shorts. He grew his hair longish and wore it swept back with pomade—another thing that set him apart. After all, in the early 1940s, the most popular hairstyle for German boys was an undercut—the hairstyle of the Hitler Youth, the Nazi Party's children's wing. And Lagerfeld—a young gay man who was interested in fashion—definitely didn't belong in the Nazi culture of his peers. His experiences soured him on childhood altogether. He told the *New Yorker* in 2007, "I hated the idea of childhood; I thought it was a moment of endless stupidity."

By 1939, Germany's aggression in Europe had sparked World War II, and the country was immersed in battle on multiple fronts until it finally surrendered in 1945. Living in a rural environment shielded Lagerfeld from the war for a while, but eventually, it came to his doorstep. When he was twelve years old, in 1945, the Allies took Germany, and his family's house was seized by the British Army. Lagerfeld, his parents, and his two sisters were ordered out at gunpoint and had to live for a year in the family barn with scarce food. The experience left Lagerfeld with a real need to leave his past behind him. Of postwar Germany, he said, "I wanted to get out of there as soon as I could." And he left, in 1952 at age nineteen, for Paris.

Fashion was Karl Lagerfeld's goal in Paris, and he enrolled in a trade school for couturiers. One of his fellow students at the school was Yves Saint Laurent, another future fashion luminary. Both Lagerfeld and Saint Laurent won in different categories of the International Wool Secretariat, a fashion design competition, in 1954. This led to Lagerfeld being hired as an assistant at Balmain—a respected couturier, but not the most glamorous one. (That honor went to the House of Dior, where Lagerfeld's classmate Saint Laurent was hired.) From Balmain, Lagerfeld moved on to another fashion house, Jean Patou, in 1959, and then in 1962, he did something unheard of: he left couture for the less prestigious

COUTURE AND READY-TO-WEAR

Couture is a kind of high-end fashion that is custom-made to fit the person who wears it. It's typically very expensive and exclusive. Ready-to-wear is cheaper, mass-produced clothing that can just be purchased from a store—no need for custom fittings for expensive fabrics. For a long time, couture and ready-to-wear were totally different worlds; couture houses didn't produce ready-to-wear, and vice versa. Designing couture was considered an art, while designing ready-to-wear was just a job.

world of ready-to-wear. He began working as a freelance designer for different houses, designing whatever they asked him to. Lagerfeld was always a hard worker, and he produced large amounts of quality work—without anyone ever attaching his name to it.

FAUX NOBLE

WHILE LAGERFELD WAS working hard at fashion, he was also working hard at his own image. He dressed up and went out on the town in heeled black patent boots, a bowtie, and a floor-length fur coat, and always had his black hair perfectly swept back. He showboated around town in a cream-colored Mercedes and flaunted his body at the Piscine Deligny, a popular place to socialize. At the pool, he wore a retro, full-body bathing suit and a pair of heels; he didn't look like anyone else there, which was exactly what he wanted. People were under the impression that he was fabulously wealthy, perhaps the heir to a fortune—a rumor *he* had started. Sure, he was starting to

IN THE MEADOWS of northern France, a winding driveway leads to a large château with pink granite walls. It looks like an eighteenth-century manor house, noble and refined. The large, wooden front door swings open, revealing a man in a suit with padded shoulders, white makeup on his face, and a monocle, with his hair gathered back into a ponytail called a catogan. But this isn't the eighteenth century: this is 1973, and the man at the door is Karl Lagerfeld.

A young Lagerfeld (second from right) and associates at Maison Chloé in Paris.

accumulate money, but it was money he had made himself, through his own hard work. Lagerfeld didn't care, though; he was creating an image of himself as cultured nobility, and the image stuck.

In 1964, Lagerfeld took on a contract that would come to define him: as a designer at the ready-to-wear brand Chloé. There, he could design fashionable clothing that lots of people would buy, without the pretensions of couture. While the job suited Lagerfeld, nobody in the fashion world took notice,

because ready-to-wear was still playing second fiddle to couture. That was one of the things Lagerfeld would change through his career.

In the 1960s, Paris was stuffier and more backward than some other world cities, but Lagerfeld himself was cultured, widely read, and fluent in English. Like many designers, he drew inspiration from the world around him, and his ready-to-wear designs were partly inspired by the students he saw walking the Paris streets. But by the late '60s, Lagerfeld needed more connection to youth culture to fuel his creativity, and so he began to develop an entourage. His entourage in 1969 mostly consisted of creative young American hippies: models and photographers who had come over from New York looking for a new adventure. Inspired by them, Lagerfeld adjusted his own look and began to dress in flowing jersey tops and bell-bottoms, with a scarf around his neck. But he also maintained an affectation of wearing high heels and carrying a clutch, which his hip young friends thought was weird. For them, Lagerfeld was the checkbook: he paid for their nights out on the town and took them on vacations to Saint-Tropez. Secretly, they made fun of him. But they were an endless source of energy for Lagerfeld. He later said, about the way he took inspiration from those around him: "I am a sort of vampire, taking the blood of other people."

In 1970, Lagerfeld met a man who was even stranger than he was: Andy Warhol. Warhol was in Paris to film a movie called *L'Amour*, and when he saw Lagerfeld and his entourage of fashionable bohemians, he cast them in his film; Lagerfeld even offered up his apartment to use for filming. Warhol had been extremely effective

MONOCLES

A monocle is a circular lens attached to a chain that corrects vision in one eye. In the late nineteenth century, monocles became a popular fashion accessory for upper-class men, often combined with a top hat and jacket. Wearing one today is considered a sign of comical pretension; a monocle means you want people to think you're rich, and you don't mind looking a little silly to prove it.

in creating a character, using clothing and style, to sell his art, which inspired Lagerfeld. In the wake of meeting him, Lagerfeld picked up a fan and a monocle, which became signature parts of his ensemble, and began showing up to meetings thirty minutes late on purpose—to cement his image as an elusive genius.

The longer Lagerfeld worked for Chloé, the less anonymous he became, even though he was still a freelancer. His edgy, commercial, and current ready-to-wear designs for the brand sold extremely well, and Lagerfeld himself was rapidly becoming a fashion personality. With

that came real money, which allowed him to acquire another accessory to enhance the aristocratic lifestyle he was building for himself: a manor house in the French countryside. It was called Penhoet, and it was built in 1756, which Lagerfeld liked to remind people was "the year Mozart was born." And then there was Lagerfeld's boyfriend, Jacques de Bascher, who had an elegance that led some people to compare him to a Parisian courtesan. Lagerfeld helped style him with winged collars and a tapered mustache, and Bascher's princely charm helped shore up Lagerfeld's aristocratic image.

STYLE AMBASSADOR

LAGERFELD CONTINUED TO quietly pump out ready-to-wear designs for Chloé and other brands throughout the '70s and '80s, clad in his heeled boots, white ponytail, and black sunglasses. In 1975, he signed a deal

to create a fragrance for Chloé and went to America to promote it. On that trip, he presented himself as the European aristocrat he had always wanted to be, wearing silk shirts, a cravat, and dark sunglasses; quoting

ABOVE THE FAST-FASHION store H&M in New York towers a giant billboard of a man wearing a trim black suit jacket, a pair of slender black jeans, and a narrow tie, with his white hair tied back in a ponytail. His expression, behind his sunglasses, is difficult to read. At 9:00 a.m. the doors to the store burst open, and a massive crowd rushes in. Minutes later, a woman walks out wearing her purchase: a T-shirt bearing the outline of that same man with the sunglasses.

Lagerfeld in his signature fingerless gloves, ponytail, and sunglasses.

the eighteenth-century writers Goethe and Voltaire to the press; and keeping large numbers of books in his suite. Americans ate it up, and Lagerfeld became an international star.

And then, in 1982, something shocking happened: Lagerfeld went back to couture. He was hired to design for Chanel, a couture house whose profits had plummeted after the death of its founder, Coco Chanel, eleven years earlier. Not only was it a sign that Lagerfeld had suddenly made it, but it was also a sign that the fashion world was ready to acknowledge the dominance of ready-to-wear. Up until

Lagerfeld took over, Chanel had been a brand known for being practical and conservative; Lagerfeld changed all that. He designed clothing with vague S&M references and put the Chanel "Cs" on everything. Some accused him of being vulgar, but his unorthodox approach worked, and Chanel became cool, relevant, and sought-after again. And for Lagerfeld, the role at Chanel magnified his fame even more.

In the '80s, a mysterious disease began spreading in the fashion world, causing people to waste away and, after some time, die. Eventually this disease was given the name AIDS.

And in late 1989, it claimed the person closest to Lagerfeld: Bascher. Lagerfeld, filled with grief, put on a large amount of weight and began dressing in flowing black robes designed by Yohji Yamamoto and powdering his hair white. He didn't have another significant relationship after that point and controversially told *Vice* magazine in 2010, "I personally only like high-class escorts. I don't like sleeping with people I really love. I don't want to sleep with them because sex cannot last, but affection can last forever."

Sartorially, Lagerfeld mourned until 2000. At that point, he decided

THE AIDS CRISIS

During the 1980s, AIDS, an autoimmune disease, became a pandemic that swept around the world. Today there are drugs that can effectively treat AIDS and HIV, the virus that causes it, but in the '80s, no such treatment existed, and catching AIDS usually meant dying. The victims of AIDS were often gay, and the disease took a massive toll on the gay community in a few short years. Because fashion was a culture that attracted a lot of gay men, the fashion world was especially traumatized by AIDS.

that his look was passé and went on a crazy diet that helped him lose ninety-two pounds, which he later promoted in a book called *The Karl Lagerfeld Diet*. He said he wanted to be able to fit into the slim suits made by the young French designer Hedi Slimane, and he achieved his goal. From then on, he was always seen in virtually the same outfit: narrow black suits or skintight jeans paired with fingerless black gloves and dark glasses. It was a look that became iconic when Lagerfeld jumped into fast fashion, producing a collaboration with chain store H&M in 2004. Lagerfeld's image was plastered all over giant billboards, and people lined up overnight for a chance to buy something from the collection. And Lagerfeld, if possible, became even more famous—like a rock star.

Post-seventy, Lagerfeld's uniform has remained pretty much consistent —so much so that he has become a popular Halloween costume. But that's just a testament to how successful he's been at creating a unique look. And

CHOUPETTE

Many famous people have famous pets, and Lagerfeld is among them. He adopted Choupette, a fluffy white Birman cat with blue eyes, in 2011. She has become extremely famous—she appears in photo shoots and has more than 100,000 Instagram followers—and Lagerfeld adores her. "There is no marriage, yet, for human beings and animals," he told CNN. "I never thought that I would fall in love like this with a cat."

the rumors he circulated have stuck, too: today, Lagerfeld is viewed as a sort of eccentric fashion aristocrat. Would he have gotten where he did without creating this complex role for himself, without turning himself into a myth? Probably not. It took a lot of hard work, but Kaiser Karl is firmly on his throne. ◆

FASHION SPOTLIGHT
JEAN-PAUL GAULTIER

FULL NAME: Jean-Paul Gaultier

BORN: April 24, 1952, Arcueil, France

OCCUPATION: Fashion designer

BAD BOY CRED: Rule-breaker Gaultier made nonconformity chic.

REBELLION IS THE central trait of designer Jean-Paul Gaultier's fashion. Often named as fashion's *enfant terrible*, Gaultier uses fashion as a tool to both shock and delight.

Gaultier wasn't born into fashion. He grew up in social housing in a working-class suburb of Paris, and he never had any formal fashion training, aside from designing clothes for his teddy bear. As a teenager, he began sending his sketches to designers and was hired by Pierre Cardin to work as an assistant when he was only eighteen, in 1970. With the help of his boyfriend, Francis Menuge, Gaultier started his own eponymous house in 1976.

Right from the get-go, Gaultier set out to change fashion's stodgy ways. While other fashion houses typically only used ultra-slender, young white models, Gaultier cast a wide array of people in his shows: models of various races, plus-size women, older men, people with lots of tattoos, and people who didn't conform to typical gender roles. At the time, this raised eyebrows, but Gaultier wasn't interested in conformity. For his designs, he took inspiration from streetwear, which in the '70s was heavily influenced by punk; one of Gaultier's first memorable creations was a stretchy nylon shirt covered with designs that looked like tattoos.

Gaultier became a major star after he met the pop star Madonna and designed a sexually provocative costume for her Blond Ambition World Tour, which involved a cone-shaped bra worn on its own, as outerwear. But Gaultier didn't limit his lingerie to women: he later designed corsets for men, too. He loved to blur gender boundaries, and one of his most infamous designs was his 1985 man-skirt. Wearing clothing typically associated with women can open men up to ridicule, and Gaultier wanted

to challenge that idea; why couldn't skirts be for men, after all? Gaultier ended up selling thousands of the designs and, even today, still includes skirts for men in his collections.

Gaultier had built his business with the help of his boyfriend, and so when Menuge died from AIDS in 1990, it was devastating for the designer. Suddenly, fashion was painful for Gaultier. He considered quitting and began dabbling in other

Gaultier in stripes, flanked by models.

Models at Gaultier's men's show at Paris Fashion Week.

things: hosting *Eurotrash*, an irreverent, surreal late-night television show that covered trends and news from Europe; and designing beautiful and bizarre wardrobes for a number of movies, including *The Fifth Element* and *The City of Lost Children*. In 1996, Dior considered him for a design job, but ultimately, Gaultier was passed over: *Eurotrash* was a little too offbeat for the brand's tastes. But that gave Gaultier the space to do something Menuge had always urged him to: launch his own couture line. It turned out that Gaultier loved working in couture, with its weird, one-of-a-kind designs,

and he still maintains the line today.

Gaultier is now a respected elder figure in the fashion establishment. He spent seven years, from 2003 to 2010, as the creative director of the high-fashion brand Hermès, and in 2011, his work was even the subject of a major museum retrospective. It's easy to see his ongoing influence, whether in gender-bending styles for men, the growing acceptance of diverse models, or the edgy fashions of designers like Rick Owens. But Gaultier isn't going anywhere, and whenever he appears in the press, even today, he gets a nod as fashion's original bad boy. ◆

ICONIC LOOK
WARIS AHLUWALIA

Designer Waris Ahluwalia's distinctive look has turned him into a fashion muse for other designers, and his recurring roles in Wes Anderson films (*The Life Aquatic with Steve Zissou*, *The Darjeeling Limited*, and *The Grand Budapest Hotel*) have made him a star. Ahluwalia's religion, Sikhism, features prominently in his dapper, dandyish style: he pairs his stylish, slender suits with a turban and beard, traditional markers of his faith.

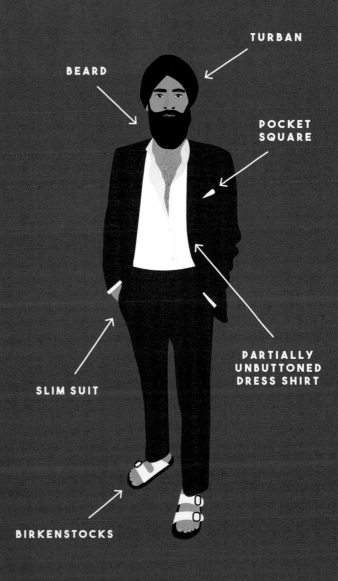

TURBAN

BEARD

POCKET SQUARE

PARTIALLY UNBUTTONED DRESS SHIRT

SLIM SUIT

BIRKENSTOCKS

CHAPTER SEVEN

CLYDE FRAZIER

FASHION ATHLETE

FULL NAME: Walter Frazier

BORN: March 29, 1945, Atlanta, Georgia

OCCUPATION: Basketball player, color commentator

BAD BOY CRED: Flashy Clyde proved that athletic prowess and daring fashion look good together.

CLYDE FRAZIER

Eyes half-closed, the man dribbles the basketball down the court—he's fast, but he looks relaxed, almost sleepy. He's wearing white short shorts and white socks with blue and orange stripes neatly pulled up to mid-calf, and on his feet are a pair of immaculately white low-cut shoes—suede Pumas with a red stripe. He's got a thick head of hair and a trimmed beard, and his jersey bears the number 10—on the back, it says FRAZIER. The crowd watches him; he's barely breaking a sweat. One onlooker turns to another: "Man, that Clyde, how does he stay so darned cool?" And then there's a swish as the ball falls through the basket.

These days, some pro athletes—particularly basketball players—are major fashion icons. Russell Westbrook, called the "king of NBA fashion" by journalists, often makes headlines for his style, and men's fashion magazines like GQ run image galleries documenting what he wears. The L.A. Lakers' LeBron James regularly sits front row at Fashion Week sporting fashionable duds. The trend is so prevalent that "top ten," "top fifteen," and "top twenty" lists of the most fashionable NBA players are seen as clickable content for blogs. But back before most of these young, stylish men were even born, the original NBA style icon was Clyde.

BORN COOL

WALT "CLYDE" FRAZIER wasn't born to the basketball court, but he wound up there pretty early. He was the eldest in a family of nine children, seven of them girls. Even as a child, he was excellent at projecting a cool image. As the oldest kid in the family, he had a lot of responsibility: he had to burp his baby sisters and change their diapers, but he knew how to spin it to his own advantage. He told the other kids in the neighborhood that, yeah, what real men do is change diapers. They believed what he said, and so it was. Frazier had so many diapers to change that he was the manliest man in town.

Frazier grew up in a lower-middle-class neighborhood in then racially segregated Atlanta, and police cars roaming the streets were a regular feature of life, but he was never much of a troublemaker. He admired his father, who was a factory worker and a fashionable dresser, and he would

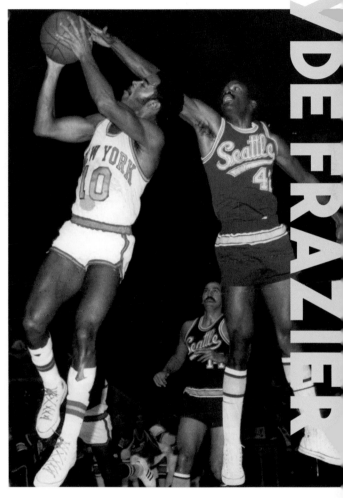

Frazier's cool moves on the court.

sneak into his father's closet to try on his clothes. But Frazier spent most of his time playing sports, and when he was nine years old, he learned to

111

play basketball on a dirt court, which was the only facility his all-black school had. The court was bumpy and full of rocks, and the ball bounced erratically—meaning Frazier had to work harder to dribble. But he was dedicated to playing well. He was dedicated, too, to looking cool, and every night he'd go home and wash his white sneakers so they'd be gleaming by the next morning.

Frazier played baseball and football, too, and by the time he was finishing high school, he had received more scholarship offers to play football than basketball. But at the time— the 1960s—the NFL was even less diverse than the NBA, and black quarterbacks were unheard of. Being black determined his fate; Frazier wanted to play in a league where he could excel, so he went for the basketball scholarship. And in 1967, the New York Knicks drafted him in the first round.

In college, Frazier had been a dapper dresser, wearing button-down shirts, skinny trousers, and penny loafers. But as soon as he was drafted, he kicked things up a notch: the first thing he did was go out and buy a pair of alligator leather shoes.

RACE AND FASHION IN THE NBA

In the 1960s, when Frazier began to play for the NBA, some thought the league had an unofficial "quota" for how many black players could play for each team. However, because teams that played black players were so successful, the rumored quota disappeared in the '70s, and black players became dominant— and black fashion styles, such as Afros and, in the 1980s, hip hop style, became accepted. For a while, anyway.

SUPER FLY

HEADS TURN AS the tall man in the long black mink coat walks into the bar. He's wearing a black, wide-brimmed gaucho hat; a black turtleneck; black tailored trousers; a gold medallion on a chain; and a pair of alligator boots. Women turn around and grab his arm as he passes; black, white, it doesn't matter—they all seem to love him. "Clyde!" the bartender calls, warmly. "You want a drink?" "Yeah, man," he replies, "I'll take a Chablis."

SUCCESS: FRAZIER LOVED it. He loved the money, he loved the women, and he loved the chance to express his personal style, which he defined as "cool." "Cool is my style," he later declared in his book, *Rockin' Steady*.

Frazier, strutting in a tailored suit.

113

He was known for not showing any emotion on the court, meaning that other players couldn't tell what he was thinking. But off the court, he let his clothing express everything for him. In his first year in the NBA, Frazier's salary was $25,000—and he spent $10,000 of that on clothing. One of those purchases was a brown velour hat with a wide brim, which he bought for $40—which translates to nearly $300 today. People, both on his

BLAXPLOITATION FILMS

Blaxploitation films were a popular genre of B movies in the 1970s. They were aimed at black audiences and relied heavily on stereotypes about African Americans. Set in poor urban neighborhoods, they usually featured heroic black characters battling some sort of enemy. Characters in these movies were usually very cool and dressed the part, audaciously and provocatively. A good example is the 1972 film *Super Fly*, whose main character, a drug dealer who is trying to escape the underworld, wears wide-brimmed hats, stylish suits, and long leather coats.

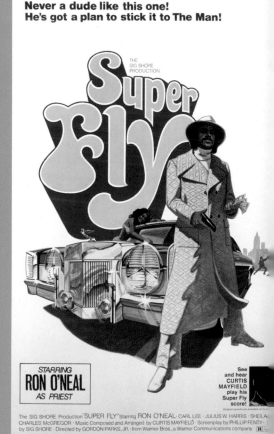

Never a dude like this one!
He's got a plan to stick it to The Man!

THE SIG SHORE PRODUCTION

Super Fly

STARRING
RON O'NEAL
AS PRIEST

See and hear CURTIS MAYFIELD play his Super Fly score!

The SIG SHORE Production "SUPER FLY" starring RON O'NEAL · CARL LEE · JULIUS W. HARRIS · SHEILA CHARLES McGREGOR · Music Composed and Arranged by CURTIS MAYFIELD · Screenplay by PHILLIP FENTY · by SIG SHORE · Directed by GORDON PARKS, JR. · from Warner Bros., a Warner Communications company

CELEBRITY SNEAKERS

The two most iconic, old-school sneaker collaborations come from Converse: Chuck Taylors and Jack Purcells. Chuck Taylor was not actually a professional basketball player—it turns out he fabricated his sports résumé and was primarily a (very successful) shoe salesman. Nonetheless, Chuck Taylors, made by Converse starting in 1932, are a sportswear classic. The real athlete-endorsed-sneaker pioneer might be Jack Purcell, a world-champion badminton player who designed a shoe for the B.F. Goodrich Company in 1935. Converse purchased the trademark to this shoe in the '70s and still manufactures it today.

Sports celebrity–endorsed sneakers really took off in the '70s, beginning with the Clyde. But the most famous is the Air Jordan, made for Chicago Bulls basketball star Michael Jordan in 1984. The shoes were so coveted that wearers were regularly robbed— one high school student was even killed by another teenager for his Jordans in 1989. Celeb sneakers are still in high demand: people line up for the release of star-endorsed sneakers like Kanye West's Air Yeezys, and shockingly, people are still sometimes robbed and killed for their shoes.

CLYDE

Walt "Clyde" Frazier

Clydes. The essence of cool.
Inspired by basketball legend Walt Frazier, these suedes let you play it cool, both on and off the court. And the choice of color combinations is virtually endless.

PUMA
Our word for quality

team and on opposing teams, laughed at him, but Frazier decided he would wear what he wanted to wear. Seeing him in his expensive hat, the team's trainer called him "Clyde," after the style worn by Warren Beatty in *Bonnie and Clyde*, a popular movie about a pair of gangsters on the run. The name stuck, and "Clyde" Frazier was born.

During his time in New York, Frazier became what the *New York Times* deemed a "New York Jock Folk Hero." He became famous—not just in New York but worldwide—for his outlandish, fashionable wardrobe of reptile-skin shoes, dramatic hats, tailor-made suits, turtlenecks, capes, and gold chains, which resembled fashion from blaxploitation films. He was also known for driving around town in a flashy Rolls-Royce. Fashion was so much a part of his life that in 1970, when a reporter named Ira Berkow was contracted by the publisher Prentice Hall to help Frazier write a basketball instructional book, Berkow realized it should be about fashion, too. Four years later, the book

Rockin' Steady: A Guide to Basketball and Cool was published. The book was a mixture of advice on basketball, lifestyle, and fashion—so popular at the time that its fans included a young Barack Obama.

By 1973, Frazier was a big enough style icon that the footwear brand Puma approached him to design a shoe. At the time, sneakers weren't considered stylish; they were shoes designed for playing sports and roughhousing, and meant for getting dirty. Nobody would have thought to pair sneakers with a pair of dress pants or wear them out for a night on the town like they do today. But the Puma Clyde changed all that. Puma offered Frazier money—unheard of at the time—not only to wear the shoe but to help design it, too. The result was a slightly wider-fitting, low-rise suede sneaker, which Frazier wore for games. The shoe quickly became popular within hip hop subculture— so popular that stories spread of the shoes getting stolen right off the feet of people wearing them.

WILD STYLE

"WE ALREADY KNOW there's going to be a lot of dishing and swishing," the TV announcer for the Knicks game says with a confident grin. His outfit is over the top: he's wearing a tailored custom suit jacket in a cowhide print, a navy shirt, and a neatly knotted tie. His curly hair is cropped close, and he's got a beard. "Yeah," he continues enthusiastically. "They've got a lot of razzle and dazzle."

Frazier, today, in one of his flashy suits.

AFTER HE RETIRED in 1980, Frazier made the jump to become an NBA commentator, first for radio and later for TV, a medium perfect for a man famous for his outlandish clothes. And Frazier stepped it up for the new job. He adopted a unique way of describing plays using rhyming phrases—"bounding and astounding," "dancing and prancing," "moving and grooving." And his wardrobe became even more flamboyant. He loved animal prints, and his custom suits included a red-and-black cow print, a leopard print, and a zebra print—though he'd sometimes go for

117

something tamer, like plain magenta. In 2010, he told ESPN that his closet was an entire room and that he owned about eighty pairs of shoes and over a hundred suits. People still can't seem to get enough, and articles about his unique style—both in the past and now—continue to be published today.

Iverson.

THE NBA DRESS CODE

Prior to 2005, style in the NBA had been getting pretty wild; Dennis Rodman dyed his hair pink and wore dresses off court, while some players channeled the energy of hip hop style. But in 2005, the NBA adopted a dress code meant to distance basketball from "thuggish" associations, becoming the first major-league sports association to do so. Things that were banned included baggy shorts, do-rags, chains, medallions, Timberland shoes, and sunglasses—that is, clothing popularized by hip hop. Players were instructed to wear "business casual" clothing (suits and slacks) instead. Some commentators thought the dress code was explicitly racist, an attempt to make a predominantly black sport more appealing to a white audience. "They're targeting my generation— the hip hop generation," said Allen Iverson, a player famous for confidently sporting cornrows, tattoos, and baggy clothing. However, over the years, some grew to like the dress code—and others credit it for the way modern players have adopted high fashion and learned how to have fun with it.

Both the sports and the fashion worlds have changed since Frazier's heyday in the '70s: off-court fashion is watched more carefully by fans due to social media, and fashionable dressing is now required. The NBA dress code means that every player needs to dress up a little, a change Frazier doesn't see as restrictive but, rather, approves of: "I think it was long overdue," he told *GQ* in 2016. "These guys are millionaires, so they should look like millionaires when they go to work." Today's players have resources that Frazier didn't: some, like Dwyane Wade and Russell Westbrook, have personal stylists who pick out their clothing and carefully tailor their looks for events. These stylists, who are familiar with the fashion industry and know what looks good, help players who want to be fashion icons break out and become famous for what they wear off court. Still, it's easy to see Frazier's influence on the dapper dressers of today's NBA. By coming first, Frazier gave them

Frazier rocking some tiger stripes.

CLYDE FRAZIER

a model for precisely how cool a basketball player could be. Whether dishing or swishing, razzling or dazzling, he's a fashion original. ◆

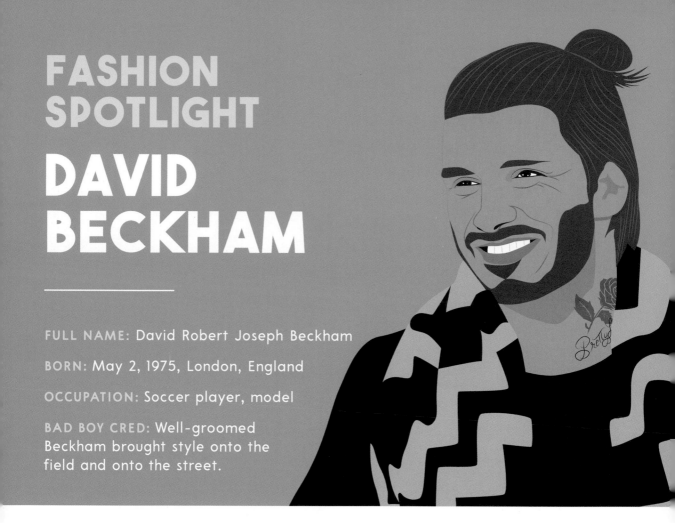

FASHION SPOTLIGHT

DAVID BECKHAM

FULL NAME: David Robert Joseph Beckham

BORN: May 2, 1975, London, England

OCCUPATION: Soccer player, model

BAD BOY CRED: Well-groomed Beckham brought style onto the field and onto the street.

MUSCULAR, AGGRESSIVE, AND brutish: for a long time, the stereotype attached to male athletes was one of macho masculinity. That is, until 1995, when a sleekly groomed, soft-spoken, and graceful man named David Beckham came to dominate European football—and become a fashion star.

Beckham was born into a middle-

class family in the suburbs of London, but his family didn't cheer for the London football teams: they were fans of Manchester United, a famously good team that played in Northern England. Beckham was excellent at soccer when he was a kid, winning competitions by age eleven—and by 1995, when he was eighteen, he was a full-time starter with his family's favorite team. A year later, he joined England's team at the World Cup.

Beckham quickly began to make headlines for his style of play; he was notorious for his ability to "bend" the ball—that is, make it curve in midair so that the person receiving it couldn't predict where it would land, a skill particularly valuable when a player is making a free kick on a goal. But it wasn't just his soccer skills that caught people's attention: it was also what he wore.

Beckham had long been interested in clothing. At age six, as the pageboy at a wedding, he was given the choice between a regular suit and "burgundy velvet knickerbockers with white tights and white ballet shoes," as he later recollected to the BBC, and he chose the latter. His peacocky sartorial choices didn't stop there. In 1997, at the World Cup in France, he caused a stir when he went out on the town with his then-girlfriend, soon-to-be-wife Victoria Adams (a member of the pop group the Spice Girls), wearing

a black tank top, sandals, and a patterned sarong—which, to most people looking at it, was basically a

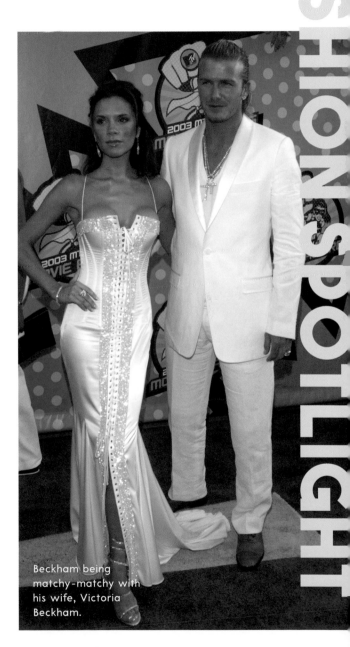

Beckham being matchy-matchy with his wife, Victoria Beckham.

Beckham's high ponytail and earrings.

skirt. That was only one example in a long series of outfits that came to define him; he and Victoria once went out in matching black leather suits, and on other occasions he wore gold pants and a metallic pink suit. He fussed with his hair, highlighting it and braiding it into cornrows, and put on nail polish. He also posed, half-naked, in a number of racy underwear ads, first for Armani and later for his own collection for H&M.

Beckham's interest in style made him one of the most famous "metro-sexuals," a term that caught on in the 1990s to define a new type of man who wasn't constrained by gender roles, at least in terms of fashion. Metrosexuals dressed well, paid attention to fitness and grooming, and were interested in nice things. Style-wise, there was little to differentiate them from many gay men, who had long been interested in male fashion and beauty. Beckham also attained a huge gay following, which he embraced: "When people talk to me about being a gay icon I think of it as a great honor," he told *GQ* in 2008.

Beckham's public enthusiasm for decidedly unmacho things—his love for his wife, his interest in fashion, his support for his gay fans—made him a trailblazer for a new kind of sports star. He used his massive fame in a traditionally masculine field to take metrosexuality mainstream. ◆

ANDRE AGASSI

During the '90s, tennis champion Andre Agassi was a massive star—not just for his incredible skills on the court but also for his wild, street-style-influenced clothing. Tennis gear was typically quite sedate, with players favoring white. But rebellious Agassi wore bright neons and crazy patterns that emphasized his individuality, topping it off with a mullet that would have looked at home in a metal band (it was actually a wig). Industry associations criticized his style, and in response, he said, "I think you should have freedom to express what you feel. Wearing colors is what tennis needs. It adds a little something. Without colors I'd still be me, but I'd be more boring."

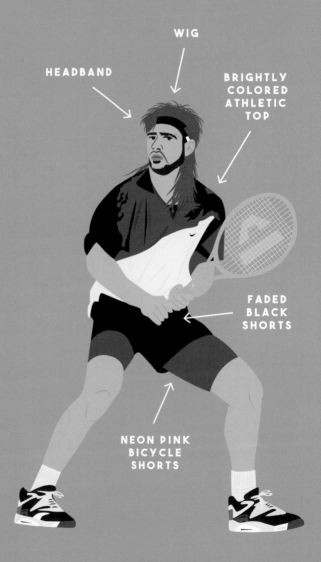

WIG

HEADBAND

BRIGHTLY COLORED ATHLETIC TOP

FADED BLACK SHORTS

NEON PINK BICYCLE SHORTS

CHAPTER EIGHT

MALCOLM McLAREN

FASHION PROVOCATEUR

FULL NAME: Malcolm Robert Andrew McLaren

BORN: January 22, 1946, London, England

DIED: April 8, 2010, Ticino, Switzerland

OCCUPATION: Fashion designer, musician, creative impresario

BAD BOY CRED: Punk puppeteer McLaren borrowed, stole, and sold underground culture to the masses.

MALCOLM MCLAREN

On a spring day in 1971, a couple sashays down King's Road in Chelsea. In this bohemian London neighborhood, the streets are lined with shops selling colorful silks, patchwork trousers, beads, and incense. But these two don't look anything like hippies. The woman wears a mohair sweater over black tights, and her white-blond hair is cut short and spiky, while the man wears a powder-blue suit that looks like something from the 1950s. They keep walking, past the throngs to a quieter, less trendy part of the street, till they get to a building numbered 430. A man stands out front, smoking, and calls out to the man with the blue suit, "Where are you going, man? I dig the drainpipes." The woman turns to her boyfriend and says, "Let's go in."

Manipulator, provocateur, pretender: over the years since he rose to fame as the manager (and creator) of the genre-defining punk band the Sex Pistols, these are just a few of the things Malcolm McLaren has been called. Whether you like him or not, McLaren was responsible for turning the youthful, anarchic fashions of punk into a worldwide phenomenon.

ROCK 'N' ROLL CHILDHOOD

McLaren with Vivienne Westwood in the '70s.

MCLAREN'S DISTRUST OF authority began when he was very young. He was born in North London into a well-to-do Jewish family; his grandparents worked in the apparel industry. But when McLaren was only two years old, his father left, and his mother largely stopped taking care of McLaren. She was a traveling saleswoman, and, newly single, she had gone what some called "man-mad" looking for a new husband. Both meant she wasn't around, and so McLaren was raised by his grandparents. Ever since, McLaren knew that the people in charge couldn't be relied upon.

McLaren hated school; "I was like a wild animal," he later said of his time as a schoolboy. But he was always a charismatic leader. When he was six, he convinced all the children in his class to skip school with him, and they squatted in a vacant lot all day until it was time to go home. Nobody figured out they'd been skipping school for a week.

By the time he was eleven, McLaren figured out another way to express himself: through clothing. He loved to dress up and had his grandfather make him a flashy turquoise suit. By the time he was thirteen, he was dressing up in suits and going to youth clubs, and by sixteen, he knew where all the hotspots were—mostly coffee bars that served as hangouts for teens.

At the time, the mod subculture—which revered modern jazz, tailored suits, and Vespa scooters—was big, but McLaren wasn't part of it; "I was there before them," he later bragged.

Given how much he hated school, it was no surprise that McLaren left it as soon as he could, at age sixteen. He got a job at a haberdasher's (a hatmaker's) and, on the side, began attending art school; he eventually enrolled full-time, rotating through a series of schools including Harrow Art School and Goldsmiths. McLaren stood out from the crowd during his art school years. He was skinny and dressed in long overcoats, and made his already-pale complexion even whiter with talcum powder. Against his pale skin, his red hair was a shocking contrast, and along with his left-wing politics, it earned him the nickname Red Malcolm. At Goldsmiths, McLaren became besotted with the work of the French Situationists, which inspired him to play subversive anti-capitalist pranks. For example, he once dressed up as Santa Claus, led a group of art students into the toy department of Harrods, and began giving away toys to random passersby.

In his art school years, McLaren met the woman who would be his most important collaborator: Vivienne Westwood. Westwood was the older sister of one of his friends, five

FRENCH SITUATIONISM

The Situationists were a group of French avant-garde artists and political revolutionaries, the most famous of whom was Guy Debord, who wrote Situationism's most important work, *The Society of the Spectacle.* Situationists believed that capitalism was bad for human society, and they used public pranks and hoaxes to turn capitalism against itself and make it look ridiculous.

years older than McLaren and a single mom fresh out of a marriage. She was creative and artistic, and made her own jewelry, which she would sell at markets. McLaren pursued her, and soon she was his girlfriend. She quickly became pregnant, and the two had a son together. They also opened up a small shop in the back of a clothing store at 430 King's Road, where they sold vintage records and clothing they had found at markets.

ROCKING THE BOAT

IT WASN'T LONG before McLaren and Westwood had taken over the whole space at 430 King's Road and named it Let It Rock. They sold clothes for a new generation of Teds, or "Teddy Boys," a youth subculture that had been popular in the 1950s. Teddy Boys wore drape jackets, skinny trousers, and string ties, and gelled their hair into ducktails—a look that had become uncool and then cool again, simply because by the early '70s, it was retro. Westwood was in charge of recreating and reinterpreting old Ted classics—over the years, McLaren supplied ideas, but Westwood was always the one who executed them.

———————

A BOAT PACKED with young people drinking beer cruises down the Thames. As it reaches the Houses of Parliament, a band begins playing right on the boat. The spiky-haired singer, dressed in a white blazer and printed T-shirt, yell-sings into the mic; his lyrics are about anarchy and apathy, including sarcastic references to the Queen. Soon, police boats surround the vessel. Seeing them, a red-haired, pale-skinned man stands up, raises a fist, and yells, "You fascist bastards!" as police pull him off the boat.

———————

But the fascination with Teds didn't last long. By 1972, they had renamed the shop Too Fast to Live, Too Young to Die, and were selling leather biker clothing festooned with zippers, inspired by Marlon Brando. In 1974, they took the leather look further and began selling their version of fetish wear, renaming the shop SEX. They called it "rubberwear for the office," and some of the things they sold included black latex pants, whips, chains, handcuffs, and screen-printed T-shirts of Snow White and the Seven Dwarfs engaging in sexual intercourse. This subversive environment attracted cool, arty young people who began to hang out at the shop, including the members of a band called The Swankers.

In 1974, McLaren wanted a new adventure, and he moved to New York. There, he began managing a proto-punk glam band called the New York Dolls. The Dolls were famous for their glammed-up, gender-bending style, which included a lot of makeup, gold lamé jackets, and

sequined top hats. McLaren outfitted them in red vinyl jeans and T-shirts

McLaren posing in Teddy Boy attire in front of his store.

(made by Westwood) and issued a "manifesto" about the band, titled "Better Red than Dead," which riffed on Communist propaganda and flew in the face of America's anti-Communist fervor. The stunt failed as a PR campaign, but it was a good example of McLaren's Situationist tactics.

While in New York, McLaren sought inspiration from the late-night music scene and would hang around Max's Kansas City and CBGB, both hot venues for the new punk sub-culture. There, McLaren spotted a man named Richard Hell. Playing in a band called Television, Hell wore ripped-up, safety-pinned shirts, leather jackets, spiky hair, and T-shirts with messages written on them, like "Please kill me." McLaren loved Hell's style: it was precisely the subversive look he imagined for the band he wanted to manage. After the New York Dolls fell apart, he tried to convince Hell

FETISH FASHION

Fetish fashion is provocative clothing often made from fabrics like leather, PVC, latex, spandex, and fishnet. Its intent is to titillate, and as such, it's not very practical: some fetish fashions restrict movement, while others expose parts of the body, such as buttocks. Until rock musicians began adopting it, it was primarily sold in sex shops.

NAZI PUNKS

In the '70s, Nazi imagery, particularly swastikas, appeared on punk clothing worn by people who were not Nazis themselves, a trend McLaren was partially responsible for. As he was Jewish, the symbolism was personal for him: he wanted to shock, but he also wanted to reject the taboos of the generation that came before him. Unfortunately, by 1978, a subgenre called Nazi punk had appeared, and punk music started to be used as a recruiting tool for neo-Nazi organizations. Today, wearing swastikas in an ironic or shocking way is uncommon because it is so easy to misinterpret the wearer's intention as support for racist causes.

to come to London to be the new frontman for the Swankers. Hell, to McLaren's frustration, said no.

But McLaren found his singer back in London: a young man named John Lydon—or Johnny Rotten—who hung around SEX. One of the Swankers convinced Lydon to come in for an audition, and he arrived with green hair, a ripped-up Pink Floyd T-shirt over which he had scrawled "I hate," and safety-pinned pants. Rotten got the job, and McLaren renamed the band the Sex Pistols—a reference to the name of his shop. He dressed the band in clothing from the shop, made by Westwood: slogan T-shirts that said things like "DESTROY" over the image of a crucifix or swastika, or "Cash from Chaos," and bondage pants covered with zippers.

The Sex Pistols began playing around London in 1976 and earned a reputation for chaos. Sometimes they would even storm the stage at venues where they hadn't been booked, and play fast, aggressive songs about anarchy, a subject

The Sex Pistols.

McLaren had convinced them to embrace. But the moment that catapulted them into the world's consciousness was in 1977, during the Queen's Jubilee—the twenty-fifth anniversary of Elizabeth II taking the British throne. The band had just released a royalty-mocking single called "God Save the Queen," and as a promotional tactic, McLaren rented a boat and sailed it down the Thames, complete with a film crew, photographers, and beer. The band was clad in their best punk fashion: leather pants, chains and padlocks, silk-screened T-shirts, and spiky hair, and when the boat stopped in front of the Houses of Parliament, the band let

McLaren with Vivienne Westwood, who wears a Sex Pistols shirt.

loose with songs like "God Save the Queen" and "Anarchy in the U.K.," both of which openly scoffed at the Queen and British society. McLaren and others were arrested, but McLaren's provocative, Situationist-style stunt paid off: the single went to number one on the charts, and the Sex Pistols were suddenly massive stars whose every public appearance promoted the styles sold at McLaren and Westwood's boutique, which was now named Seditionaries. The Sex Pistols disbanded in 1978 due to fighting within the band and with McLaren, but they made an indelible mark on both fashion and music.

BORROWING AND STEALING

IN THE PUB, the TV screen flickers with a music video. In it, a woman and four men dance in rhythm together. All four of them wear blousy, romantic shirts and billowy pants, and the men carry boom boxes on their shoulders. The woman wears a jaunty pirate hat, and she sings about cassette tapes. In the bar, a red-haired man stands and watches, and then turns to the spiky-haired woman beside him. "Let's take this fucking pirate look to the catwalk!" he exclaims.

AFTER THE SEX PISTOLS, McLaren had earned a reputation as a brilliant (though manipulative) provocateur, and others sought out his management, including a young punk named Adam Ant, who had a band called Adam and the Ants. McLaren agreed to manage them, but he was skeptical of Adam as a lead singer. So he persuaded the Ants to leave Adam—not the most polite move. (Adam went on to stardom on his own.) McLaren recruited a fourteen-year-old girl, Annabella Lwin, to be the band's singer, and together they became known as Bow Wow Wow. At the time, McLaren was obsessed with a new technology: cassette tapes. He was interested in the idea of piracy, and he wrote lyrics for Bow Wow Wow about taping songs off the radio (which the record labels frowned upon). His fascination with pirates extended into fashion, too. At the time, Westwood was designing a collection centered on romantic fashions of the French Revolution; McLaren suggested that he wanted the clothes to look more

CASSETTE TAPES

In the 1950s and '60s, music was sold on records, large vinyl discs that played music but couldn't re-record it. In the late '70s, a newer technology became popular: cassette tapes. Cassettes were small and portable, meaning listeners could carry their music with them and play it outside the home, first on larger players called boom boxes and later on Walkmans with earphones. Most importantly, cassettes allowed people to record music off the radio or from other sources—a development that made record companies angry, because they didn't want people to be able to get music for free.

like pirate clothes. The result was the Pirate collection, which was released under 430's new name: Worlds End. McLaren dressed Bow Wow Wow in the pirate clothes, and the collection was McLaren and Westwood's first major international success.

Following the Pirate collection, McLaren grew less involved with Worlds End, and eventually, he and Westwood split in a bitter dispute. By 1983, McLaren was no longer involved in Westwood's collections, and she went on to become a respected high-fashion designer of punk and historically influenced clothing, which she sold under a label bearing her name. McLaren, meanwhile, continued to appropriate and rebrand other cultures: he recorded his own albums, which borrowed heavily from African music and hip hop, and even recorded an album of reinterpreted opera songs.

McLaren was controversial to the end of his life. His last words before he died from mesothelioma in April 2010 were "Free Leonard Peltier" (in reference to the Indigenous American activist who was imprisoned for allegedly shooting an FBI officer, and whom many human rights organizations consider a political prisoner). At McLaren's funeral, his casket, spray-painted with the words "Too Fast to Live Too Young to Die," was lowered into a grave, which would later be marked with a gravestone emblazoned with "Better a spectacular failure, than a benign success"—the motto McLaren lived by.

McLaren didn't invent punk; Richard Hell, Johnny Rotten, and many others were living it before McLaren claimed it as his own. But what McLaren did was pull it from the underground into the mainstream. He repackaged it for public consumption and acted as its chief publicist. After McLaren's stunt on the Thames, the world knew what punk fashion looked like, and anarchy became a topic of dinner conversation, while his collaborations with Westwood transformed fetish wear into something you might find at the office. At a show dedicated to his work at New York's New Museum in 1998, he described his career this way: "I think it can be summed up, as it often is in the press, as being a very bad boy." ◆

FASHION SPOTLIGHT

KURT COBAIN

FULL NAME: Kurt Donald Cobain

BORN: February 20, 1967, Aberdeen, Washington

DIED: April 5, 1994, Seattle, Washington

OCCUPATION: Musician

BAD BOY CRED: Cobain's nonconformist style defined a generation.

IN THE '90S, grunge fashion was everywhere; from high school hallways to high-fashion magazines, oversized flannel shirts, ripped sweaters, and baggy jeans dominated. And the man who was mostly responsible —reluctantly so—was Kurt Cobain.

Cobain grew up in Aberdeen, Washington, as an only child, and when he was nine, his parents divorced. Cobain was deeply unhappy about the split, and as his parents pursued new relationships, he became rebellious. Eventually, he found refuge in punk music. The first album he bought was by The Clash, but for Cobain, the Sex Pistols were a bigger influence: in his teenage journals, he called them "one million times more important than the Clash." He started attending shows by a band called the Melvins and, through them, became involved in the local music scene. He also became involved with the feminist punk riot grrrl scene in Olympia, and his friendships there, including with people like Bikini Kill frontwoman Kathleen Hanna, helped cement his commitment to gender equality.

Cobain's band, Nirvana, fused elements of punk, metal, and hardcore to create what became known as grunge music. After the release of *Nevermind*, which contained the massive hit "Smells Like Teen Spirit," Nirvana became a sensation: they were the biggest band of the '90s. Their fame made Cobain a celebrity, and the way he dressed was copied by millions. His style

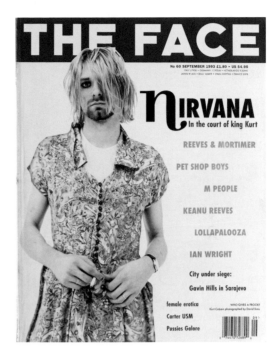

Cobain on the cover of *The Face* in a dress.

was antiestablishment, gender non-conforming, and influenced by the cold weather of the Pacific Northwest and Cobain's own poverty. He layered baggy, torn cardigans; band T-shirts; flannel pajama tops; and jeans; and dyed his hair punky colors with Kool-Aid. He adopted elements of women's fashion, like dresses and nail polish, and famously wore a prim, floral-print button-up dress on the cover of the magazine *The Face*. The way he dressed was a message to the band's fans, and to the world, about his politics. He wrote in the liner notes of *Incesticide*, "If any of you in any way hate homosexuals, people of different color, or women, please do this one favor for us—leave us the fuck alone! Don't come to our shows and don't buy our records."

Cobain suffered from depression and drug addiction, and struggled with the burdens of fame. He hated rock music's macho culture and at one point said that he would prefer to play backup in Hole, the band led by his wife, Courtney Love, rather than continue as the frontman of Nirvana. Tragically, he committed suicide at age twenty-seven, and the grief felt by his fans—millions of them—was intense. Cobain's death was one of the most significant events of the era, and today, he's still feted as an icon. His style endures, too: high-end labels like Saint Laurent and Raf Simons have released recent collections modeled after Cobain; but if you really want to

Cobain, Courtney Love, and daughter Frances Bean.

nail the grunge look, you'd be better off shopping at a second-hand store—like Cobain did. ◆

ROBERT SMITH

As the frontman for The Cure, Robert Smith perfected a style both moody and emotional. The Cure became popular in the post-punk era of the late '70s and early '80s, when dark, dirgey goth rock was emerging as a style, accompanied by morbid, all-black wardrobes and heavy makeup that made the wearer look cadaverous. Though Smith claims his band isn't goth— "I just play Cure music, whatever that is"—he's an undeniable goth style icon.

BACKCOMBED BLACK HAIR

HEAVY EYELINER

LIPSTICK

OVERSIZED BLACK CLOTHES

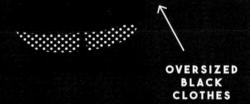

CHAPTER NINE

DAVID BOWIE

FASHION ROLE-PLAYER

FULL NAME: David Robert Jones

BORN: January 8, 1947, Brixton, South London, England

DIED: January 10, 2016, Manhattan, New York, New York

OCCUPATION: Singer, songwriter, actor

BAD BOY CRED: Bowie's over-the-top, androgynous fashion blurred the lines of what menswear could be.

DAVID BOWIE

The sea of people at the Hammersmith Apollo gaze toward the stage, swaying in ecstasy. They all look oddly alike: many of them have fire-engine-red or bright-orange hair cut into a spiky hairdo that's short in the front, longer in the back. The man onstage commanding their attention holds a guitar and wears a metallic suit with pointy shoulders that jut out in a futuristic way. His hair, like theirs, is a bright shock of red, and his skin is pale, verging on translucent. The expression on his face is distant and removed, like an alien dreaming of home. And then he stops playing his guitar and speaks into the mic. "Of all the shows on the tour this particular show will remain with us the longest, because not only is it the last show of the tour, it's the last show we'll ever do."

The reaction is immediate. Some people start crying. Some of the redheads gasp and embrace one another. Others start yelling. "Ziggy! Ziggy, nooooo!"

Shape-shifting musician David Bowie was a visionary artist whose ability to predict trends (and start them) gave him a career that spanned more than four decades. A multitalented musician and actor, Bowie used his strong aesthetic sensibilities to create characters that transcended his own identity, shaping popular culture along the way.

THE BOY WHO FELL TO EARTH

WHILE BOWIE'S LIFE was marked by its theatricality, young Bowie's childhood was as unremarkable as they come. He grew up in postwar England in the suburbs of London, in a small, working-class house. As a child, he loved rock 'n' roll music and idolized the fashionable, showman-like rock star Little Richard. His older brother, Terry, had a record collection, and through him, Bowie discovered jazz. When he was fourteen, he had his parents buy him a saxophone, which he dreamed of playing in the band for a jazz great like Charles Mingus or John Coltrane. By age sixteen, he was playing his sax in a group called The Konrads. But it wasn't until his next band, at age seventeen, Davie Jones and the King Bees, that he began to toy with his image. He would appear onstage dressed a little like Robin Hood, in knee-high suede boots with

Bowie in 1969, the year "Space Oddity" was released.

tassels, with bright-yellow dyed hair. He stood out from the other musicians of the era, who favored simple blue jeans. But there was one way in which he didn't stand out: he shared a name with Davy Jones, the leader of the popular band The Monkees. And so Davie Jones renamed himself: suddenly, he was David Bowie. Under that name, he released an album full of songs of pop psychedelia, but it was largely unsuccessful. For the next two years, he didn't make any more music.

But he did do something very interesting instead: he began to study under Lindsay Kemp, a famous English dancer and mime. Kemp taught Bowie how to create a stage persona, and he taught him how to move. Kemp's influence was obvious in the next song that Bowie released: "Space Oddity." Released in July 1969, five days before the launch of the Apollo 11 moon mission, the song

ANDROGYNY

In the 1960s, gender boundaries were very clear: men were supposed to dress like men, and women were supposed to dress like women, and being gay, or bi, or anything but straight was not socially acceptable (and, in fact, had only just become legal). Bowie very publicly embraced ambiguity in his gender presentation: he wore dresses and makeup and sometimes wore his hair long. He told the press different things about his orientation: that he was gay, and that he was bisexual, and eventually that he was straight. Regardless of his orientation and gender presentation, he exuded sexuality and virility, proving that it wasn't necessary to be "masculine" to be a man.

tells the story of a character played by Bowie named Major Tom, an astronaut who becomes lost in space. The song became a hit, but people had no expectations for Bowie to produce more music. "Space Oddity" was viewed as a novelty. But Bowie would prove everyone wrong.

For his next album, *The Man Who Sold the World*, Bowie began to experiment on another frontier: gender. He appeared on the cover of that album in a long, flowing dress, a so-called man's dress created by a designer called Mr. Fish. To Bowie's displeasure, the cover art was considered too controversial to be included in the American release—in those days, it was almost unheard of for a man to dress in women's clothing, and the American market was more conservative than the British one. But when he was in the States to promote the album, he got his way, appearing for his interviews in a dress. As he told *NME*, "It's a pretty dress. I had to go to Texas so I thought I'd test the reaction. One guy pulled out a gun

and called me a fag. But I thought the dress was beautiful."

Soon after that, Bowie applied what he'd learned from Kemp and began working on a character: a sexually charged alien rock star named Ziggy Stardust. With the help of a designer, Freddie Burretti, he designed outrageous suits inspired by two futuristic movies that were popular at the time—*2001: A Space Odyssey* and *A Clockwork Orange*. He also cut his hair into an avant-garde mullet and dyed it bright cherry red. And so Ziggy was born. Bowie created an entire album, *The Rise and Fall of Ziggy Stardust and the Spiders from Mars*, to tell Ziggy's story. He toured, dressed completely in character, and people began to believe that Bowie *was* Ziggy. As Ziggy, Bowie became massively famous and was one of the main instigators of glam rock, alongside Marc Bolan. He developed the character further on his next album, *Aladdin Sane*, which memorably featured Bowie with a painted lightning bolt on his face; the image was so iconic that the *Guardian* referred to it as "The Mona Lisa of album covers."

As Bowie's fame increased, his costumes grew more and more elaborate, some of them inspired by the Japanese art of Kabuki, a kind of Japanese theater featuring stylized dance, wild wigs, dramatic costumes, and distinctive white, black, and red makeup. Soon, he had hired the Japanese designer Kansai Yamamoto to design outrageous custom outfits for him. Bowie's adoring fans would dress up like him at his shows (and for some of them, all the time). And that's why when Bowie announced that his show at the Hammersmith Apollo in 1973 was his last one, his fans freaked out. Their idol was gone. Or was he?

SLENDER MAN

AFTER BOWIE RETIRED Ziggy, he left the U.K. for America—making the split official. In New York, he recorded an album called *Diamond Dogs*, inspired by the dystopian novel *1984* as well as by Bowie's own vision of an apocalyptic future. His last stab at glam rock, the album featured a grotesque painting of a half-dog, half-man Bowie on its cover. His next album after that, *Young Americans*, was music that he dubbed "plastic soul," which borrowed heavily from African American soul and R&B.

Soon after, he moved to Los Angeles and began to adopt a new persona: thin, pale, dressed in a suit, with groomed blond hair. On its surface, the look might have seemed conservative, but Bowie had borrowed it from androgynous German cabaret stars like Marlene Dietrich and had been inspired by the excesses of Weimar cabaret. And the persona was wild, too; named the Thin White Duke, he was a sort of crazy aristocrat.

INSIDE A DARK house in Los Angeles, a man sits cross-legged on the floor, facing a woman. The man is wearing a tailored suit, a white button-up shirt, a vest, and leather shoes, and his ice-blond hair is slicked back. He gazes at a series of esoteric-looking tarot cards. "Hmmmm," the man says. "Very interesting." "I'm getting tired of this, David," says the woman. "Can't we eat now? You're looking awfully skinny." "I'm not hungry," he replies. "Maybe I'll have some milk."

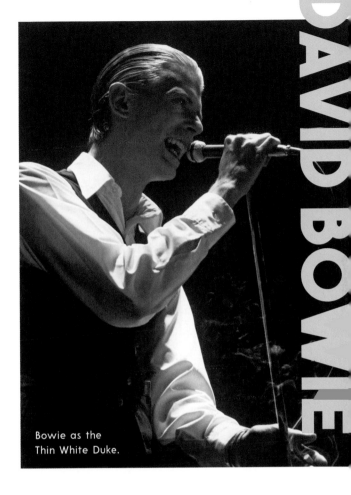

Bowie as the Thin White Duke.

The character became controversial because when Bowie appeared in public during this era, he said a number of pro-fascist things. He later claimed it was only theater, part of the character, but it could have been something else, too.

While Bowie was in America, he developed a very bad addiction to the stimulant drug cocaine. He was so openly addicted that, in 1975, the British press had no qualms about referring to him as "old vacuum-cleaner nose." The drug made him extremely paranoid, and he became fascinated by magic and the esoteric arts, like the works of occultist Aleister Crowley, tarot cards, and Kabbalah.

His diet only consisted of cocaine, red peppers, and milk, and he was becoming both crazy and emaciated. It was in this state of mind that he filmed the movie *The Man Who Fell to Earth*, in which he played an alien. It was also when he recorded *Station to Station* and officially debuted as the Thin White Duke. But Bowie couldn't live like that—paranoid, obsessed with the dark arts, undernourished, and losing his mind—forever. "I was out of my mind, totally crazed," he later said of the time. And so, to get a fresh start, he moved to Berlin.

In Berlin, Bowie moved in with another musician, Iggy Pop. Away from the hard-drug scene of L.A., he kicked his cocaine habit. And there, he recorded what was known as his "Berlin Trilogy" of albums: *Low*, *"Heroes,"* and *Lodger*. His sound of this era was influenced by the pared-down, mechanical German Kraut-rock genre, which included bands like Kraftwerk. While he was there, he also starred in a movie, *Just a Gigolo*, in 1978, in which Dietrich made her final appearance.

WEIMAR CABARET

Between World War I and World War II, the government of Germany was known as the Weimar Republic. Flush with postwar funds and relaxed social norms, the Germans partied hard and enjoyed their newfound freedom. In this environment, cabarets became popular. Weimar cabaret featured themes of sex and politics, and the scene was considered to be quite debauched. One of the most famous roles played by film star Marlene Dietrich—as a gender-bending cabaret singer who wore a suit and kissed another woman—was inspired by Weimar cabaret.

OUT OF CHARACTER

AFTER A DECADE of taking on personas, Bowie decided he was done with playing dress-up. His 1980 album, *Scary Monsters*, was a goodbye to the '70s and all his characters: Major Tom, Ziggy, and the Thin White Duke. But Bowie did play one more character, albeit briefly: in the video for "Ashes to Ashes," he rounded up a bunch of club kids from London and dressed up as Pierrot, an Italian pantomime figure who was a fashion reference point for the New Romantic subculture. After that, he mostly stuck to the straight-and-narrow path when it came to his appearance. "The outfits I use on stage now are far more functional," he said at the time. There were no more characters. Unless you count the movies. In 1986, Bowie took on one of his most memorable movie roles: Jareth the Goblin King in the movie *Labyrinth*, in which he wore a long, bejeweled jacket; a white silk

The Goblin King, played by Bowie, in *Labyrinth*.

TWO YOUNG MEN stand in the crowd, watching the man with orange hair. He stands onstage with his back to everyone, wearing a knee-length frock coat. The coat is ripped and tattered, and printed with a familiar design—the Union Jack, the flag of the United Kingdom. "Hey, that's an Alexander McQueen design," one man says to the other. Just then, the band starts playing and the man onstage spins around, grabs the mic, and starts singing.

shirt with a ruffled collar; polished boots; and a dramatic blond mullet.

By the 1990s and 2000s, Bowie was an established rock icon, but he didn't stop experimenting with his sound or his look. His 1995 album, *Outside*, integrated industrial dance music, which was then popular, into its sound. And Bowie found a modern fashion muse, too. In 1996,

he read something in a fashion magazine about a young designer named Alexander McQueen. He liked the designs, and so he gave him a call. Would McQueen design costumes for Bowie's tour? The answer, of course, was yes. In fact, McQueen had been inspired by Bowie, too; the clothing in his 1996 collection had been partially modeled on Bowie's role in a vampire movie called *The Hunger*. The Union Jack frock coat McQueen designed for the Earthling Tour ended up being an iconic piece featured in museum displays, and Bowie's showcasing of McQueen's designs on two tours helped the designer become a massive star. The two, collaborating, brought each other's art to a higher level. In the 2000s, Bowie experienced a similar circular influence with the designer Hedi Slimane. Bowie admired Slimane's slim suits for Dior Homme and had the designer dress him. But there was a reason why Bowie found that aesthetic so appealing: Slimane's designs had been inspired by Bowie's look in *The Man Who Fell to Earth*.

Bowie's dedication to performance lasted right to the very end of his life, and even beyond. In early January 2016, he released an album called *Blackstar*—the release date was his sixty-ninth birthday. The music video for the first single, "Lazarus," featured Bowie lying on his deathbed, and included lyrics about being in heaven. Two days after the album was released, Bowie died from liver cancer—a condition he had kept a secret. The world was shocked. But soon, people began interpreting the album, which featured themes about death, as an extended goodbye to fans. It made sense that a man who had lived life as a performance would turn his death into a performance, too.

Bowie's cultural influence has reverberated through the decades and shows no signs of stopping. His inspired characters informed shape-shifting performers like Madonna and Lady Gaga, and his androgyny helped blur the boundaries of the gender binary and reshape what, exactly, it was acceptable to wear. He created glam rock and inspired the subculture of New Romantics. In the wake of his death, multiple designers released collections in honor of Bowie; it's easy to imagine him, looking down from above, admiring the designs and claiming them as his own. ◆

NEW ROMANTICS

A reaction against the anti-fashion, hard-edged look of punk, the New Romantic subculture was inspired by Bowie and his glam rock style. New Romantics wore androgynous clothing in historical styles (like frilly English Romantic shirts and 1930s cabaret styles) as well as cosmetics. Famous New Romantics included Boy George and the band Duran Duran.

FASHION SPOTLIGHT
PRINCE

FULL NAME: Prince Rogers Nelson

BORN: June 7, 1958, Minneapolis, Minnesota

DIED: April 21, 2016, Chanhassen, Minnesota

OCCUPATION: Singer, songwriter, record producer

BAD BOY CRED: Sartorially daring Prince made music a whole lot sexier.

TO CALL THE cover of Prince's 1980 album, *Dirty Mind*, provocative may be an understatement. Dressed only in an open trench coat, a neckerchief, and black bikini briefs, bare-chested Prince poses coyly, with a seductive gaze; his eyes are rimmed with eyeliner, and he's got a mustache, too. Throughout his life, Prince's look, which straddled the masculine and the feminine, was unabashedly sensual. Like Bowie, he was an icon of androgynous style.

Prince was born in Minneapolis, Minnesota, to musical parents. His dad led a jazz band, and his mom was a singer. Prince picked up music early; he taught himself how to play piano at age seven and supposedly wrote his first song, called "Funk Machine," at that precocious age. By the time he was fourteen, he had also taught himself how to play guitar and drums, and joined a band called Grand Central (later called Champagne), in which he played guitar. The band was serious; they often skipped school in order to practice. But Prince's time in the band came to a close when, at age seventeen, he recorded a demo that landed him a contract with a record company by the time he was eighteen.

Prince's musical ability was unmatched. Not only did he play multiple instruments, but he wrote, produced, and performed all his own songs, often playing all the musical parts. His sound blended funk, pop, rock, and other influences; it was so creative, it was hard to pin down. And right from the beginning, his lyrics were sexually suggestive; with Prince, everything was erotic. So, too, was his look.

Prince's iconic style was defined by the 1984 film *Purple Rain*. In it, Prince played a stylized version of himself called The Kid. The Kid wore frilly shirts, stacked heels, a shiny purple suit, lace gloves, and a halo of curls. He had a skinny mustache, and his features were accentuated by makeup. He looked like a sexed-up dandy, and he had a backup band, The Revolution, that he styled to match him. Both the

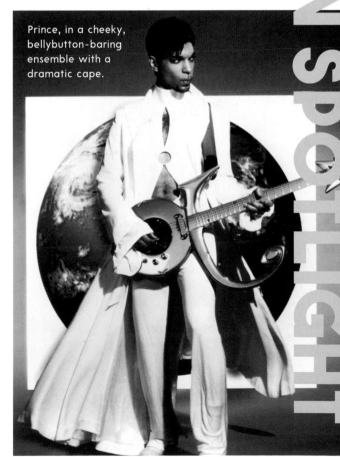

Prince, in a cheeky, bellybutton-baring ensemble with a dramatic cape.

film and the album, which included hits like "Purple Rain" and "When Doves Cry," made Prince a massive international star. His soundtrack for the movie *Batman*, which included the song "Batdance," further cemented his fame. And a temporary name change, to an unpronounceable symbol that blended the male and female symbols, added to his notoriety.

Prince maintained an androgynous, sexually provocative look throughout his career, which spanned thirty-nine albums over almost as many years. While purple was his signature color, nothing was off-limits sartorially. Some of his more flamboyant outfits included a yellow lace suit cut low into a V at the front, with the trousers cut like chaps to reveal his buttocks, which he wore to the 1991 MTV Video Music Awards; a fringed black suit that ended in the middle of his abdomen, leaving the top part of his torso bare, which he wore at a concert in 1990; and a low-cut, white silk suit complete with a hood, which he wore at the People's Choice Awards in 2005.

When Prince died from an accidental pain medication overdose in 2017, people around the globe reacted with shock. Nobody can really step into His Purpleness's stacked heels, but his influence lives on. In a moving statement on how Prince has changed the world, singer Frank Ocean said, "He made me feel comfortable with how I identify sexually simply by his display of freedom from and irreverence for obviously archaic ideas of gender conformity." ◆

ICONIC LOOK
LITTLE RICHARD

Rock 'n' roll icon Little Richard's look and sound paved the way for other flamboyant, performance-oriented musicians, like James Brown, Prince, and Bowie. A pioneer of the early days of rock music, Little Richard's wild performances on the piano were known for bringing together black and white audiences; he played to mixed crowds in the days when racial segregation was still the norm. And Little Richard's over-the-top outfits, which included feminine flourishes like blouses and makeup, pushed the boundaries of what a man could wear.

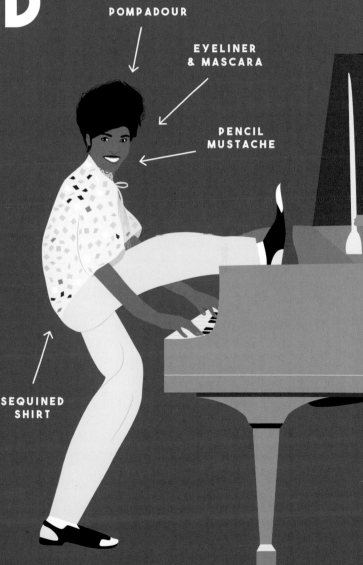

POMPADOUR

EYELINER & MASCARA

PENCIL MUSTACHE

SEQUINED SHIRT

CHAPTER TEN

KANYE WEST

FASHION IDEALIST

FULL NAME: Kanye Omari West

BORN: June 8, 1977, Atlanta, Georgia

OCCUPATION: Rapper, producer, fashion designer

BAD BOY CRED: High-minded Kanye brought sensitivity and intellect to hip hop's sound and aesthetics, while his ego brought him infamy.

KANYE WEST

In a studio in Midtown Manhattan in the year 2000, two men are talking. One wears baggy pants low on his hips, an oversize basketball jersey, and a ball cap with the brim to the back. The other wears a fitted pink polo shirt, tailored trousers, Italian leather shoes, and a ball cap with the brim to the front. The guy with the pink shirt has a Louis Vuitton backpack sitting on the table beside him, CDs spilling out of the open zipper. He's gesturing and talking loudly with a Midwestern accent. "Listen, man, I can rap!" he says. "You don't know it, but I'm gonna be a star." And with that, he starts rapping, an intense expression on his face. The other man in the baggy pants stares at him, amused. "I dunno, man," he says. "You're a producer. Why don't you just produce?"

Kanye West: these days, he's a megastar known as much for his ego as his revolutionary reshaping of hip hop. But West's confidence in his own talent was what elevated him from a middle-class kid with dreams of stardom to a lauded musician—and may be what brings him success in fashion, too.

THE WONDER YEARS

RIGHT FROM THE beginning, West was raised to be special. His father was a photographer with strong opinions who was involved with the Black Panthers, while his mother, Donda, was an ambitious intellectual with a master's degree who held down three jobs to buy the family a house. When the two had their only son, they named him Kanye, a Swahili word meaning "the only one." Only eleven months after West was born, his parents separated, and two years later, after the divorce was finalized, his mother moved with him to Chicago, where she'd raise him mostly as a single mother—a deeply supportive one.

West was a strong-willed child; at one point, he insisted that ducks were quacking the wrong way. He was a fiend for attention—when he was six years old, he lip-synched to Stevie Wonder songs in talent competitions, dressed, in full costume, as Stevie himself.

Kanye with his mom, Donda.

Music and style were undeniable passions for West by the time he was twelve. He performed in an amateur dance troupe called Quadro Posse and took on the role of manager and stylist, dressing the whole group in black. Donda caught him posing in the mirror in his outfit, saying to himself, "I could be a teenage sex symbol."

Not long after that, at age thirteen, West started a rap group called State of Mind. Their first song was called "Green Eggs and Ham" (yes, named after the Dr. Seuss story), and West acted as the group's producer, engineering the recording. Thrilled with the experience, West began saving money to buy real production equipment, like samplers and drum

Run-DMC.

EARLY HIP HOP STYLE

The hip hop look of baggy clothing, sportswear, and sneakers began with Run-DMC, a pioneering rap crew who grew famous in the early 1980s and whose embrace of Adidas track suits and shoes defined streetwear for years to come. The aesthetic was later shaped, in the mid-'80s, by the ascendance of gangsta rap, a hard-hitting style of music pushed forward by artists like Ice-T and N.W.A. Gangsta rap's tough image was influenced by criminal gangs like the rival Crips and Bloods, who wore blue and red bandannas and the jackets of different sports teams to declare their allegiance. But from the beginning, hip hop was also tied to aspirational displays of wealth through expensive designer fashion and "bling" (flashy jewelry), a look that was referred to as "ghetto fabulous."

machines. Seeing his talent, his mother splurged and bought him a keyboard. She helped him in another way, too: one of her coworkers at the university was the mother of a hip hop producer named No I.D. (who, at the time, was working with rapper Common), and Donda managed to wrangle an introduction for her precocious son. By age fourteen, West had a legitimate home production studio, and he also had a mentor. From then, his path was set.

By fifteen, West was a recognizable face on the Chicago rap scene—but he was still a typical teenager. He had braces, wore then-stylish low-slung baggy pants, and carried a backpack. When he started showing an interest in brand-name fashion, like Calvin Klein, he was teased for being "gay"—the hip hop scene at the time was homophobic, and an interest in fashion wasn't something that was welcomed or that fit rap's gangster image. West was undeterred, though. He played into his preppy look, taking a job at the Gap—he hated

JESUS PIECE

A Jesus piece is a kind of jewelry that usually features a gold chain with a likeness of Jesus —sometimes studded with diamonds or other gems— hanging off it. It's a common hip hop accessory; rappers famous for wearing a Jesus piece include Biggie Smalls, Sean Combs, Rick Ross, Jay-Z, Ghostface Killah, Big Sean, and, of course, Kanye West.

it, but it influenced his wardrobe, and he began mixing clothes from the Gap with items from Polo Ralph Lauren.

When West graduated from high school, he went to college for a while to study art and then English. But he was distracted by music; his production career was taking off. In his self-driven style, he was approaching rappers to try to sell them beats he'd written—and eventually sold one for $8,800, a sum that he spent in its entirety on a Jesus piece and more Polo clothes. And then he scored even bigger—getting the chance to produce a track on Jermaine Dupri's album. It went platinum. In response, West dropped out of college for good in 1998, at age twenty: it was the only way he could truly concentrate on music. But Donda, who was worried, made him a deal: West had to become successful in hip hop within a year.

And he was successful. By 1999, he was producing for Roc-A-Fella Records, a label launched by rapper Jay-Z. And while he made beats that everyone loved, what West really wanted to do was rap. But nobody would let him. West, with his middle-class background and preppy fashions—he wore Gucci loafers, sports shirts and sports jackets, and tailored trousers, and

———————

A GROUP OF hipster guys wanders through New York's East Village in 2007. One wears an accessory that none of the rest have: white plastic sunglasses that look like window shutters. As they pass a clothing store, one of them stops at a sunglass rack. "Should I get some Kanye glasses, too?" He grabs a pair of neon-green shutter shades in his hand, and his friends laugh. "Whatever, man," scoffs the first guy. "I had mine before you guys had even heard of Ye."

———————

if he wore a baseball hat, the brim was turned forward—did not fit the typical gangster mold that hip hop marketed at the time. The label heads, including Jay-Z himself, just couldn't see geeky Kanye as a star.

THE BIRTH OF YEEZUS

BY 2001, WEST was a superstar—behind the scenes, anyway. He was a producer on Jay-Z's sixth album, *The Blueprint*—an album that went double-platinum and has been lauded as one of the best hip hop albums of all time. That success made his name as a producer. And yet, West's image problem persisted. He was still stylish, still preppy, and carried his demo mixtape in his Louis Vuitton backpack. And nobody would let him rap.

But then, something dramatic happened that changed everything. One night in 2002, West was at the studio late doing production work for other acts. He left about 3:00 a.m., got into his rented Lexus—and fell asleep at the wheel. When he crashed head-on into another car, it nearly killed him. Two weeks later, even though his jaw was still wired shut, West wrote and recorded a song

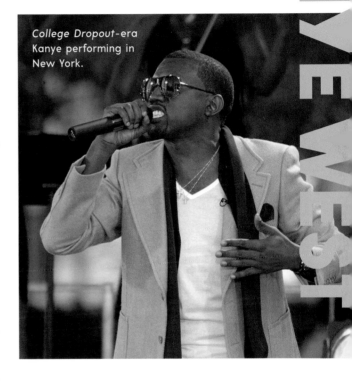

College Dropout-era Kanye performing in New York.

called "Through the Wire," in which he rapped about his experience. The inventiveness of the song, and the positive response it received, finally convinced the label execs to give him a chance.

The result, which came out in 2004, was the album *The College

Dropout, which broke the mold of typical rap at the time; one critic referred to it as "post-thug." West rapped about higher education, consumerism, and even his own spirituality—paving the way for so-called sensitive rappers like Drake and Kid Cudi. West also found another avenue for his aesthetic passions in making music videos for his songs, which he carefully art directed. The album was a huge success, and suddenly, West was a trendsetter. The preppy look was hot. (Drake later rapped about how West defined the era with his polos and backpacks.) That same year, West launched his own label, G.O.O.D. Music, which allowed him to develop other artists who shared his style of conscious rap.

Becoming a star did nothing to abate West's ego. In 2004, he freaked out at the Grammys because he didn't win the award for Best New Artist, and he notoriously went off-script at a Hurricane Katrina relief performance, telling audiences, "George Bush doesn't care about black people." But his egotism helped develop his artistry. He started thinking of himself as a brand, like Disney or Coca-Cola, and considered "opulence" and "quality" to be part of that brand. He wanted to make a great pop album, like what era-defining pop star Michael Jackson had done in the '80s and '90s, and by the time he was recording his third album, *Graduation*, he was taking cues from the type of rock music that was popular enough to fill stadiums. The album was still cerebral: the lead single, "Stronger," included quotes from the philosopher Nietzsche, and the album art was done by the artist Takashi Murakami. Its most noticeable impact, however, was on fashion. For the "Stronger" music video, West had eyewear designer Alain Mikli design a pair of custom shutter shades, plastic glasses with louvered slats rather than glass lenses. The impractical glasses sparked a major trend, and soon they could be found absolutely everywhere.

GETTING SERIOUS

IN LATE 2007, West endured a tragedy when his mother died from complications from surgery, prompting him to take life more seriously. He broke off an engagement with his then-girlfriend and, striving to take his music to a new level, experimented with Auto-Tune, which disguised his voice. West began taking fashion more seriously, too. He sat in the front row at Fashion Week shows in Paris and Milan in 2008, teasing the press by announcing that he was starting a fashion line called "Pastelle." (The line never launched.) Later that year, he said he wanted to intern at a fashion house like Louis Vuitton or Raf Simons—an audacious concept, since interns are typically low-paid twentysomethings looking for experience at the start of their careers, not mega-famous rap stars. That didn't faze West, though, and by the middle of the following year, he did score an internship—not in high fashion but at his old stomping grounds, the Gap.

West's ego may have been the thing propelling him to greatness, but it finally got the best of him in 2009. At the MTV VMAs, when Taylor Swift was accepting her award for Best Female Artist, he burst onstage, took the mic away from her, and said, "Yo Taylor, I'm really happy for you, imma let you finish, but Beyoncé had one of the best videos of all time . . . one of the best videos of all time!" Despite West's intentions—that Beyoncé be recognized for her genius—his actions made him look like a bully. He was

Adidas Yeezy Boost 350 V2s.

booed offstage, and, feeling like a pariah, he disappeared from public for the next year.

While some people might have taken time to recover after a shameful public spectacle, resting just wasn't in West's nature, and instead, he took refuge in fashion. This time, he managed to score an internship in high fashion at the Italian design house Fendi. He didn't receive special treatment: it was, in fact, a nine-to-five office job. He told a radio station, Hot 97, that it involved "every day, going to work, walking to work, getting cappuccinos!" After that experience, he recorded another album, titled *My Beautiful Dark Twisted Fantasy*, which was so critically acclaimed that the public largely forgave (though never forgot) his antics. The album featured a cover by Riccardo Tisci, a designer who was then the creative director of Givenchy. That same

Kanye sitting front row at New York Fashion Week.

THE CROWD IS hushed, and the lights are dimmed. Ten rows of models of all different sizes, genders, and ethnicities stand silently, wearing a range of muted, minimalist clothing. And then West's voiceover begins: "I see all these people commenting, 'Why's he still trying?' I mean, if I see something, if I see an opportunity, I'm gonna go for it. I'm here to crack the pavement and make new grounds, sonically and socially, culturally."

year, West made a very controversial style choice: he replaced his entire row of bottom front teeth with gold and diamond versions, revealing them in an appearance on *The Ellen DeGeneres Show*, where the host reacted with shock that, yes, these were his new teeth.

Over the years, West had a number of serious relationships, but in 2012, he finally got the girl he really wanted: socialite Kim Kardashian, who stars in a reality show called *Keeping Up with the Kardashians* and maintains a selfie-heavy social media presence largely geared toward promoting her own life. With their combined notoriety, the two became a power couple. West played stylist with her, and he continued to push the envelope with his own style, too: famously, in late 2012, he performed a concert wearing a leather Givenchy skirt. As he put it in the magazine *Paper*, "When I saw this kilt, I liked it. I was into it. It looked fresh to me. I felt creative; I didn't feel limited by some perception." Once again, West was mocked for his style,

GRILLS

A grill is a type of jewelry, typically gold and sometimes studded with gems, worn over the front teeth. Rappers like Raheem the Dream made them popular in the early '80s, and they experienced a resurgence with Southern rappers, like Nelly, in the 2000s. Grills are usually removable, unlike West's gold teeth.

and once again some people accused him of being "gay," but his embrace of gender-fluid fashion clearly had an effect: following his example, rappers like Young Thug and Jaden Smith wear skirts and dresses without shame. West later recalled the skirt as the moment he crossed over to become a fashion insider.

Perhaps that crossover was what gave him the confidence to finally launch his fashion line, Yeezy, in 2015—a collaboration with Adidas.

KANYE'S TWEETS

In 2010, Kanye West joined Twitter, and ever since, the site has been a platform for some of his most notorious braggadocio. Here are just a few examples:

I jog in Lanvin JULY 28, 2010

I always misspell genius SMH! The irony! NOVEMBER 2, 2010

You may be talented, but you're not Kanye West. JULY 6, 2012

You have distracted me from my creative process JANUARY 27, 2016

Mark Zuckerberg invest 1 billion dollars into Kanye West ideas FEBRUARY 14, 2016

#2024 DECEMBER 13, 2016

the being formally known as Kanye West I am YE SEPTEMBER 29, 2018

The streetwear and shoe collection, which debuted in New York with a fashion presentation that verged on performance art, got mixed reviews, but with each season, West continues to work on his craft, and Yeezy shows no signs of retiring from fashion.

West, however, still battles his demons. In 2016, he had to postpone part of his Saint Pablo Tour, in support of his album *The Life of Pablo*, after he appeared unhinged onstage, cutting short a performance to rant about Facebook, Jay-Z, Hillary Clinton, and Beyoncé. He was hospitalized for "temporary psychosis." His next big controversy came in May 2018, when he suggested on TMZ that black people were responsible for slavery (he apologized, emotionally, several months later). But ups and downs, wild and sometimes regrettable statements, and soaring ambitions are the status quo for West. In December of 2016, he tweeted (after a controversial meeting with President-Elect Trump) that he intended to run for president in 2024. Though he deleted the tweet, he never fully dropped the idea. And you never know. Kanye, the man nobody thought could be a rapper, proved everyone wrong once. It could happen again. ◆

SENSITIVE RAPPERS

Ye laid the groundwork for a new generation of conscious rappers whose lyrics channel complex emotions.

Clockwise from left:
Chance the Rapper,
Kendrick Lamar, Kid Cudi,
Drake, J. Cole.

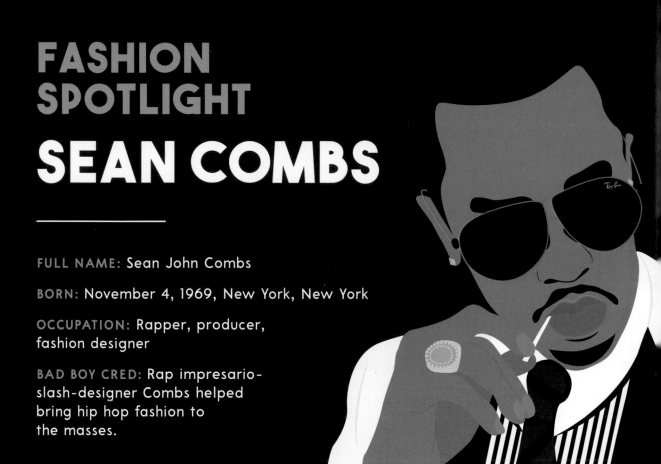

FASHION SPOTLIGHT

SEAN COMBS

FULL NAME: Sean John Combs

BORN: November 4, 1969, New York, New York

OCCUPATION: Rapper, producer, fashion designer

BAD BOY CRED: Rap impresario-slash-designer Combs helped bring hip hop fashion to the masses.

WHETHER YOU CALL him Puff Daddy, Puffy, P. Diddy, Brother Love, or Love, Sean Combs has been shaping both rap and fashion since the early 1990s. Born in Harlem, Combs studied business at the historically black Howard University in Washington, D.C., in the late '80s, where he threw weekly parties that made him a campus celebrity. Later in university, he decided to take his music promotion to the next level, and his friend Heavy D got him a meeting with Uptown Records, where the aggressively ambitious Combs begged for an internship. He commuted four hours a day from D.C. to New York to work the unpaid job, eventually dropping out of school in 1990 so he could pursue his career more seriously.

While he was at Uptown, Combs was working on his own label, which he called Bad Boy Records. He was eventually fired from Uptown over tensions about the time he was spending on his own pursuits, and he found distribution through another label, Arista. And that's when things took off for Combs. He signed acts like the Notorious B.I.G., Craig Mack, 112, and Faith Evans—all of whom were massively successful, partially due to Combs's ear for talent, and partially due to his marketing acumen.

Bad Boy's biggest star ended up being Combs himself. In 1997, after years of working as a promoter and producer behind the scenes (much like West), Combs released his first rap album, *No Way Out*, under the name Puff Daddy. It went to number one on the charts, won awards, and made Puffy a star.

And over the years, Combs proved to be a master of crafting his public image. As a performer, he perfected an early style that played up his wealth and success—slick suits in all black or all white, stylish sunglasses, gold jewelry, and leather, a polished take

Combs showing off his style at one of the biggest events in fashion, the Met Ball.

on hip hop's long-standing fascination with designer duds. He later ditched the bling, claiming it was "cheesy."

Combs, as ambitious as he was, decided to capitalize on his status as a fashion influencer. In 1998, he launched Sean John, his own fashion label, which relied on audacious advertising campaigns starring Puffy himself. The designs, which some dubbed ghetto fabulous, were meant to reflect the aspirational, multi-cultural fashions of the youth of the era: high-end athletic wear that riffed on street fashion, a precursor to the athleisure trend. "We wanted to give them fashion that represents them. We wanted to give them extremely multicultural and diverse fashion," Combs said of his intentions. And Anna Wintour, the editor in chief of *Vogue*, quietly reinforced his status as a name in fashion the following year, when she featured him in a fashion story about Paris's couture collections, publishing dramatic photos of a dapper-looking Combs posing with supermodel Kate Moss.

In 2006, Combs stopped releasing albums to focus mostly on fashion and other business endeavors—but the world was reminded of his successes in 2017 with the documentary *Can't Stop, Won't Stop: A Bad Boy Story*, all about Combs and his label. In the surrounding press engagements, Combs proved he could still surprise, telling media he'd changed his name to Brother Love—and then just Love.

Whatever he calls himself, his name still looms large: Sean John racks in more than $400 million in sales per year, and is available every-where. Combs's influence is felt in other ways, too. With his swagger, self-confidence, and fashion sense, Combs paved the way for other hip hop fashion moguls, like West. As Combs told the *Washington Post*, "I got a message from Kanye West the other day: 'Look, you're all over my mood board!' When I'd do a collection, I'd do a mood board and put everyone who inspired me on my board . . . and now I'm on other people's mood board. It's humbling." ◆

ICONIC LOOK
THE NOTORIOUS B.I.G.

The Notorious B.I.G. (born Christopher Wallace, and also known as Biggie Smalls or, simply, Biggie) was one of the most influential rappers of all time. In his songs, he played up his larger-than-life image by rapping about his fame, success, and wealth, and he dressed the part, favoring lots of bling and expensive brands, particularly Versace. Donatella Versace has even publicly acknowledged how he increased her brand's recognition. He was murdered in a drive-by shooting in 1997, forever immortalizing his look from his final album, *Life After Death*, where he favored a dapper style influenced by 1940s gangsters—a visual claim to his own hard-as-nails identity.

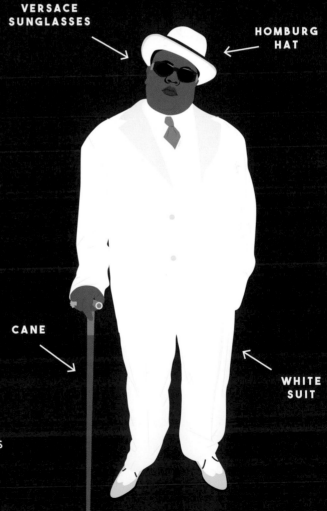

VERSACE
SUNGLASSES

HOMBURG
HAT

CANE

WHITE
SUIT

CONCLUSION

THE MEN IN this book led lives that were daring and different—and all of them used clothing to get what they wanted. Louis XIV, a mighty French king, used fashion to cement his existing power, while black revolutionary Malcolm X used it to seize the power he deserved. Writer Oscar Wilde used fashion to live a beautiful life, and punk impresario Malcolm McLaren capitalized on fashion's ability to provoke with ugliness. Basketball player Clyde Frazier proved that style could impress both on-court and off, while actor Marlon Brando rejected fashion, only to find that his bad-boy aesthetic sparked a decades-spanning trend. Artist Andy Warhol and fashion designer Karl Lagerfeld both used fashion to create characters that came to define them in life, while androgynous musician David Bowie did the same thing onstage. And then there's rapper Kanye West, whose intellectual pursuit of fashion helped him claim an identity as a creative genius.

Sure, clothes are just clothes, but they're also powerful symbols that shape how the world sees us. And men are some of the most creative and expressive dressers out there. Whether making a colorful twist on a tailored suit or bending gendered expectations by wearing a skirt, the bad boys in this book prove how the clothes make the man—whatever type of man he chooses to be. ◆

REFERENCES

CHAPTER ONE

DeJean, Joan E. *The Essence of Style: How the French Invented High Fashion, Fine Food, Chic Cafés, Style, Sophistication, and Glamour.* New York: Free Press, 2005.

Dunlop, Ian. *Louis XIV.* New York: St. Martin's Press, 2000.

GQ. "The Madiba Shirt." December 6, 2013. https://gq.co.za/culture/entertainment/the-madiba-shirt-16537920.

Kremer, William. "Why Did Men Stop Wearing High Heels?" *BBC*, January 25, 2013. http://www.bbc.com/news/magazine-21151350.

Mansel, Philip. *Dressed to Rule: Royal and Court Costume from Louis XIV to Elizabeth II.* New Haven: Yale University Press, 2005.

Stancati, Margherita. "Nehru's Tailor on Dressing a Prime Minister." *Wall Street Journal*, March 3, 2013. https://blogs.wsj.com/indiarealtime/2013/03/03/nehrus-tailor-on-dressing-a-prime-minister.

CHAPTER TWO

Craik, Jennifer. *Fashion, The Key Concepts.* New York: Berg, 2009.

Croll, Jennifer. *Fashion That Changed the World.* Munich: Prestel, 2014.

Ellmann, Richard. *Oscar Wilde.* New York: Viking, 1987.

Lubitz, Rachel. "Men in Hollywood Are Finally Learning to Embrace the Power of a Colorful Suit." *Mic*, February 6, 2018. https://mic.com/articles/187814/men-in-hollywood-are-finally-learning-to-embrace-the-power-of-a-colorful-suit#.UuAnPeuTY.

Sicha, Choire. "Donald Glover, the Only Dressed Man in Hollywood." *New York Times*, September 18, 2017. https://www.nytimes.com/2017/09/18/fashion/donald-glover-suits-emmy-awards.html.

Vasiliev, Zhenia, and Adam Frost. "Oscar Wilde's Most Enduring Epigrams—Infographic." *Guardian* (International edition), November 27, 2012. https://www.theguardian.com/culture/graphic/2012/nov/27/oscar-wilde-epigrams-quotes-infographic.

CHAPTER THREE

Biography.com editors. "James Dean Biography." Biography.com website, April 27, 2017. https://www.biography.com/people/james-dean-9268866.

Guralnick, Peter. *Last Train to Memphis: The Rise of Elvis Presley.* Boston: Little, Brown, 1994.

Hopkins, Jerry. *Elvis: The Biography.* Medford: Plexus Publishing, 2014.

Kanfer, Stefan. *Somebody: The Reckless Life and Remarkable Career of Marlon Brando.* New York: Alfred A. Knopf, 2008.

Riley, Stevan, dir. *Listen to Me Marlon.* New York: Passion Pictures Productions, 2015. Film.

Sebag-Montefiore, Clarissa. "From Red Guards to Bond Villains: Why the Mao Suit Endures."
   BBC, November 2, 2015. http://www.bbc.com/culture/story/20151007-from-red-guards-to-bond-
   villains-why-the-mao-suit-endures.

CHAPTER FOUR

BBC. "Historic Figures: Che Guevara (1928–1967)." Accessed February 28, 2018.
   http://www.bbc.co.uk/history/historic_figures/guevara_che.shtml.
Kallen, Stuart A. *Che Guevara: You Win or You Die.* Minneapolis: Twenty-First Century Books, 2012.
Lewis, Tim. "Carol Tulloch: 'Dressing Well Is Almost Part of the DNA in the Black Community.'"
   Guardian (International edition), March 6, 2016. https://www.theguardian.com/books/2016/mar/06/
   carol-tulloch-black-style-the-birth-of-cool-interview.
Malcolm X and Alex Haley. *The Autobiography of Malcolm X.* New York: Grove Press, 1965.
Rawlings, Nate. "Malcolm X and the Nation of Islam: Eve Arnold's Quietly Powerful Portraits."
   Time, February 20, 2012. http://time.com/3502682/malcolm-x-and-the-nation-of-islam-eve-arnolds-
   quietly-powerful-portraits.
Ziff, Trisha, and Luis Lopez, dir. *Chevolution.* Los Angeles: Red Envelope Entertainment, 2008. Film.

CHAPTER FIVE

Bockris, Victor. *The Life and Death of Andy Warhol.* New York: Bantam, 1989.
Haden-Guest, Anthony. "Burning Out." *Vanity Fair*, April 2, 2014.
   http://www.vanityfair.com/news/1988/11/jean-michel-basquiat.
LaBouvier, Chaédria. "The Meaning and Magic of Basquiat's Clothes." *Dazed*, February 16, 2017.
   http://www.dazeddigital.com/fashion/article/34691/1/jean-michel-basquiat-fashion-and-sense-of-style.
McCorquodale, Sara. "How Warhol's Work Influenced Our Wardrobes." *BBC*, April 27, 2015.
   http://www.bbc.com/culture/story/20150427-soup-cans-that-changed-fashion.
Quito, Anne. "Artist Takashi Murakami's Goofy Octopus Costume Is a Manifesto About Creative
   Resilience." *Quartz*, February 7, 2017. https://qz.com/903978/japanese-artist-takashi-murakamis-
   goofy-octopus-costume-for-his-new-show-at-the-chicago-museum-of-contemporary-art-is-a-
   manifesto-about-creative-longevity/.

CHAPTER SIX

Ahluwalia, Waris. "You Don't Get a Fee for Being on a Moodboard." *Guardian,* March 18, 2017.
   https://www.theguardian.com/fashion/2017/mar/18/actor-designer-waris-ahluwalia.
Drake, Alicia. *The Beautiful Fall: Lagerfeld, Saint Laurent, and Glorious Excess in 1970s Paris.* Boston:
   Little, Brown, 2006.
Orlean, Susan. "Fantasyland: Jean-Paul Gaultier's Inspirations." *New Yorker*, September 26, 2011.
   http://www.newyorker.com/magazine/2011/09/26/fantasyland-susan-orlean.

Orth, Maureen. "Kaiser Karl: Behind the Mask." *Vanity Fair*, May 15, 2008. http://www.vanityfair.com/magazine/1992/02/lagerfeld199202.

CHAPTER SEVEN

Beckham, David. *David Beckham*. Exeter, United Kingdom: Headline, 2013.

Cashmore, Ellis. "David Beckham: Rise of the Metrosexual." *CNN*, May 17, 2013. http://www.cnn.com/2013/05/17/opinion/beckham-metro-symbol.

Frazier, Walt, and Ira Berkow. *Rockin' Steady: A Guide to Basketball and Cool*. Chicago: Random House, 2010.

Klemesrud, Judy. "Clyde." *New York Times,* February 16, 1975. http://www.nytimes.com/1975/02/16/archives/clyde-walt-fraziers-lifestyle-may-be-even-more-extraordinary-than.html?_r=0.

Schneider-Mayerson, Matthew. "'Too Black': Race in the 'Dark Ages' of the National Basketball Association." *International Journal of Sport and Society* 1, no. 1 (2010): 223–33. http://www.academia.edu/225008/_Too_Black_Race_in_The_Dark_Ages_of_the_National_Basketball_Association.

Telegraph. "David Beckham Recalls Velvet Knickerbocker Outfit on Desert Island Discs." January 28, 2017. http://www.telegraph.co.uk/news/2017/01/28/david-beckham-recalls-velvet-knickerbocker-outfit-desert-island.

Walker, Randy. "Andre Agassi's Influencing Fashion Statement from 25 Years Ago." *World Tennis Magazine*, June 1, 2015. http://www.worldtennismagazine.com/archives/11903.

Wilson, Jamie. "NBA's 'No Bling' Dress Code Prompts Racism Accusations." *Guardian* (International edition), October 31, 2005. https://www.theguardian.com/world/2005/oct/31/usa.americansports.

Woolf, Jake. "Walt 'Clyde' Frazier Is Still the NBA's Greatest Style God—and He Knows It." *GQ*, October 6, 2016. http://www.gq.com/story/walt-clyde-frazier-puma-sneakers-style.

CHAPTER EIGHT

Atkinson, Nathalie. "Kurt Cobain's Fashion Choices Were Never About What to Wear, but Rather How to Wear Items on Hand." *National Post*, April 5, 2014. http://nationalpost.com/life/fashion-beauty/kurt-cobains-fashion-choices-were-never-about-what-to-wear-but-rather-how-to-wear-items-on-hand.

Bromberg, Craig. *The Wicked Ways of Malcolm McLaren*. New York: Harper & Row, 1989.

Dhillon, Kam. "10 Current Fashion Trends That Kurt Cobain Did First." *Highsnobiety*, February 28, 2017. http://www.highsnobiety.com/2017/02/22/10-fashion-trends-kurt-cobain.

Westwood, Vivienne, and Ian Kelly. *Vivienne Westwood*. London: Picador, 2014.

Williams, Zoe. "The Talking Cure." *Guardian* (International edition), June 12, 2004. https://www.theguardian.com/music/2004/jun/12/popandrock1.

CHAPTER NINE

Beaumont, Mark. "Life Before Ziggy—Remembering David Bowie's Early Years." *NME*, January 12, 2016. http://www.nme.com/blogs/nme-blogs/david-bowie-the-early-years-763372.

Broackes, Victoria, and Geoffrey Marsh. *David Bowie Is*. London: V&A Publishing, 2013.

Elan, Priya. "Prince: How His Androgynous Style Influenced Fashion." *Guardian* (International edition), April 22, 2016. https://www.theguardian.com/fashion/2016/apr/22/prince-how-his-androgynous-style-influenced-fashion.

Rolling Stone. "David Bowie Bio." Accessed February 28, 2018. http://www.rollingstone.com/music/artists/david-bowie/biography.

Rolling Stone. "Little Richard Bio." Accessed February 28, 2018. http://www.rollingstone.com/music/artists/little-richard/biography.

The Quietus. "The Fall to Earth: David Bowie, Cocaine and the Occult." January 11, 2016. http://thequietus.com/articles/07233-david-bowie-cocaine-low.

CHAPTER TEN

Beaumont, Mark. *Kanye West: God and Monster*. New York: Overlook Press, 2015.

Caramanica, Jon. "The Agony and the Ecstasy of Kanye West." *New York Times*, April 10, 2015. https://www.nytimes.com/2015/04/10/t-magazine/kanye-west-adidas-yeezy-fashion-interview.html?_r=0.

Hyland, Véronique. "Kanye's Show Was Crazy in All the Right Ways." *The Cut*, February 12, 2015. https://www.thecut.com/2015/02/kanyes-show-was-crazy-in-all-the-right-ways.html.

Givhan, Robin. 2016. "They Laughed When Diddy Launched a Fashion Line. Then He Changed the Industry." *Washington Post,* April 23, 2016. https://www.washingtonpost.com/lifestyle/style/they-laughed-when-diddy-launched-a-fashion-line-then-he-changed-the-industry/2016/04/21/d779d27e-eb99-11e5-bc08-3e03a5b41910_story.html?utm_term=.bb377b3e3136.

Gwilliam, AJ. "Biggie's 10 Greatest Fashion Moments: What Died & What Lived On." *Highsnobiety,* September 18, 2014. http://www.highsnobiety.com/2014/09/18/notorious-big-fashion-what-died-what-lived/.

Kennedy, Gerrick D. "Bad Boy for Life: A Look Back at the Rap Empire Sean 'Puff Daddy' Combs Built." *Los Angeles Times*, November 5, 2015. http://www.latimes.com/entertainment/music/posts/la-et-ms-sean-p-diddy-combs-bad-boy-entertainment-retrospective-20151005-story.html.

ACKNOWLEDGMENTS

Thank you to the unstoppable Colleen MacMillan, who cornered me at a Christmas party to demand I write a follow-up to *Bad Girls*. Here it is! Paula Ayer: I'm so glad you agreed to edit this. I'm supremely grateful, as always, for your brilliance.

Aneta Pacholska, your illustrations made this bad boy particularly handsome, and Emma Dolan, I love your bold design. Antonia Banyard, thank you for your top-notch photo research.

Kaela Cadieux, you did an expert job of steering this project through the editorial process, and I appreciated all your smart suggestions. DoEun Kwan, thank you for your careful copyedit, and Dawn Loewen, I am thrilled we were able to snag the sharpest proofreader in the land.

Rick Wilks and everyone else at Annick: thank you for your ongoing enthusiasm for all things Bad and for providing such a great home for this book.

And my final thanks go to the Canada Council for the Arts, who generously funded the writing of this book.

CREDITS

INDEX

ABOUT THE AUTHOR AND ILLUSTRATOR

Photo credit: Rebecca Blissett

JENNIFER CROLL's first fashion statement as a frog-catching, street-hockey-playing tomboy was pairing gingham dresses with pants with ripped knees. But by high school, her look had evolved to include a lot of black, and her interests included going to punk shows and writing bad poetry. Today, her signature accessory is a pair of glasses, the result of years staying up reading past her bedtime.

Jennifer has published three other books: *Fashion That Changed the World* (Prestel, 2014), about the cultural influences on fashion through history; *Bad Girls of Fashion* (Annick Press, 2016), about women who rebelled using fashion; and *Free the Tipple* (Prestel, 2018), a cocktail book inspired by iconic women.

Jennifer lives in Vancouver, Canada, with a sharply dressed tuxedo cat named Ollie.

ANETA PACHOLSKA was born in Poland and has traveled the world learning and perfecting her craft. The influences and experiences that she gained while traveling from country to country are expressed in her illustrations. From Berlin to Granada to her current home in Toronto, Aneta loves engaging with people, culture, and music—it helps her illustrate from different angles and show various perspectives. Aneta contributes a unique perspective through her distinctive illustrations, international background, and ability to tell visual stories.